TUNE UP YOUR TEACHING &
TURN ON STUDENT LEARNING

What I'm impressed with is that this book has a lot to think about, but it's a light read. So many books get mired down in the technical language that the message gets lost, or they're so boring no one finishes reading them—*not this book*!

—**Dr. Marilyn Marquand**, Retired Teacher, Site Administrator, and Science Specialist for the San Diego County Office of Education.

When I first started teaching Earth Science, I was told, "Students are 'consumers.' They don't think and don't want to think. Give them a worksheet, and they will be compliant and get their work done." Drs. Jurchan and Downing have reawakened my passion to bring out the best mysteries of the earth sciences and help students *wonder* and *experience the awe* in this field—to expand the galaxy of their life-long learning as they engage the majesty of how the Earth works, came to be, and fits into the universe.

—**David Youngblood**, Professional Science Educator, Liberty Charter High School

The analogy in this book, the archipelago of knowledge where the Monarch's goal is to get the subjects to want to explore and have their own experiences vs. have a set of pat answers regarding content seems contradictory to the current test culture in education. There seems to be a *disconnect* between learning and assessment. Your analogy illustrates the *value of teaching inquisitiveness and enabling students to access resources,* both books and peers, for their own "adventure in learning." I'm glad you're doing this work!

—**Traci Bianchi**, Coach and Parent

Most teachers spoon feed their students answers to the questions they ask them. This, in turn, never allows the students to learn and discover the answers for themselves. Dr. Downing, on the other hand, used the methods described in this book, in his classes. I apply those methods to classes I take. Those methods have become the way I will learn for the rest of my life. For that, I am very grateful. Everyone who reads this book will discover how they can help students truly learn.

—**Bailey Benson**, High School Senior

I'm reminded of two boys who came in to complain and wiggle a way out of your class. In fact, I believe one parent came in and spoke with the Principal several times. By mid-semester, both students couldn't thank me enough as the counselor for "forcing" them to stay in the class. They believe they have been placed in a better position educationally by being exposed to your teaching styles and methods, which are brought to life in this book. Just thought I would share [with your readers].

—**Dawn Roppe**, High School Counselor

All my teachers have always told me the answer when I had a question. You didn't. You made me figure it out for myself, among other things. And for that I want to thank you. You have given me a glimpse of what the real world is going to be like. Because of you and your class I am more confident in myself. I feel more independent. You prepared me well for my high school years, and many years in the future. This book, filled with strategies and rationale for what you do as a teacher, is sure to help other teachers be more effective as they help their students become better learners.

—**Rachel Seymour**, Freshman,
California Polytechnic State University, San Luis Obispo

This book reminds me that, although it may be frustrating at times to not have the answer always in front of you, it is definitely more rewarding when you've struggled with a difficult problem by yourself or with a group of peers and finally reach that "Aha!" moment. Not only do you remember what you learned much better, but you also learn how to think critically for yourself, which is ultimately one of the best things you can hope to achieve from school.

—**Hannah Youngwirth**, Senior, University of California, San Diego

When you read this book, you might find yourself constantly nodding in agreement or laughing in enjoyment! Dr. Jurchan and Dr. Downing truly understand what it means to be a professional, reflective educator, and they effectively share what they have learned in over seventy years (combined) in education. I hope that this book truly is, as they write, a catalyst for some trail blazing in education.

—**Sara Chai**, Science Educator, Montgomery Middle School,
Sweetwater Union High School District

I really want this book to be successful so that you can go out and do teacher workshops!

—**Elena McComas**, Retired Science Teacher
and Professor of Education

TUNE UP
YOUR TEACHING &
TURN ON
STUDENT LEARNING

*Move From Common to Transformed
Teaching & Learning in Your Classroom*

Dr. JoAnn Jurchan &
Dr. Chuck Downing

NEW YORK

TUNE UP YOUR TEACHING & **TURN ON** STUDENT LEARNING
Move From Common to Transformed Teaching & Learning in Your Classroom

© 2015 Dr. JoAnn Jurchan & Dr. Chuck Downing.

Published in New York, New York, by Morgan James Publishing. Morgan James and The Entrepreneurial Publisher are trademarks of Morgan James, LLC. www.MorganJamesPublishing.com

The Morgan James Speakers Group can bring authors to your live event. For more information or to book an event visit The Morgan James Speakers Group at www.TheMorganJamesSpeakersGroup.com.

BitLit

A FREE eBook edition is available
with the purchase of this print book

CLEARLY PRINT YOUR NAME IN THE BOX ABOVE

Instructions to claim your free eBook edition:
1. Download the BitLit app for Android or iOS
2. Write your name in UPPER CASE in the box
3. Use the BitLit app to submit a photo
4. Download your eBook to any device

ISBN 978-1-63047-144-6 paperback
ISBN 978-1-63047-145-3 eBook
ISBN 978-1-63047-146-0 hardcover
Library of Congress Control Number:
2014933862

Cover Design by:
Chris Treccani
www.3dogdesign.net

Interior Design by:
Bonnie Bushman
bonnie@caboodlegraphics.com

In an effort to support local communities, raise awareness and funds, Morgan James Publishing donates a percentage of all book sales for the life of each book to Habitat for Humanity Peninsula and Greater Williamsburg.

Get involved today, visit
www.MorganJamesBuilds.com

Habitat for Humanity®
Peninsula and
Greater Williamsburg
Building Partner

DEDICATION

We both dedicate this book to...

The wonderful students and colleagues (fellow teachers and administrators) who have assisted in *our* successful journey *from common to transformed teaching.*

Personal Dedications

Dr. Jurchan: To my daughter, Sasha—faith, joy, and love today and forever.

Dr. Downing: To my wife, Leanne and my granddaughter, Hadley Marie.

TABLE OF CONTENTS

PREFACE

Thank you for reading our book, and thank you even more for reading this Preface. If you are doing this because we asked you in Chapter 1 to read it if you'd skipped it, thank you even more!

- **Teachers**. We wrote this book first and foremost for *you*—elementary, middle, and high school teachers—all grades, all subject areas. However your school is configured, this book is for *you*.
- **Pre-Service Teachers**. If *you* are a pre-service teacher, we're convinced *you* will be a better student teacher and a better teacher once under contract by incorporating principles from this book in your teaching from the start. In fact, if *you* begin your professional career with these principles as **your norm**, your voice will carry more influence because of your students' achievements. Additionally, *you* won't be easily swayed by educational trends and fads that will certainly come along.
- **Administrators** and **Teacher Leaders**. Whether *you* are a principal, assistant principal, district level curriculum specialist, teacher on special assignment, or any other level of teacher in leadership,

implementation of the principles in this book will benefit those under your supervision and guidance.

- **Parents/Guardians.** *You* are in partnership with *all* of the above stakeholders. Regardless of the grade level of your child, as you read this book, we hope you will be thinking, "This is good stuff. How can I assist the teacher in implementing these ideas?"

Regardless of your tenure, you will find both theory and practical application that will help and motivate you to transform your teaching and learning environments.

While we wrote this book in a less formal style, *so you will read it*, we want you to understand that the principles we advocate are soundly based in educational theory and research. If you are skeptical, please check the list of *nearly* **eighty** sources used to validate our information and claims. You can find that list in **References** at the end of the book. In addition, the list of **References** is segregated following every chapter with a list of sources introduced in that chapter.

Other key features of this book:

- We begin our presentation of content with **The Analogy**, which will encourage you to examine your teaching practices and begin to critically analyze their efficacy.
- We included examples from core content areas that show how you can *transform common activities* into hotbeds of student thinking.
- To clarify critical points and raise questions we think many of you will have, we included "**He Said/She Said**" dialogues between the two of us. These intentionally give you insight into our thought process.
- The figures in this book are all original by the authors. Many include graphics drawn specifically for the chapter topics. Those graphics are the artistic products of two of Dr. Downing's former high school students who experienced and embraced the learning principles described in this book while in his classes.

- The tables incorporated include information that is either exclusive to that table or summarizes key points in the text... so don't skip over them.
- An access code to our website is printed in the Online Resource section of this book. It allows you to post on the Discussion Board and view/download files of resource materials.

This **Preface** provides a real-life classroom example of how good teaching methods transcend grade levels. Too many times, teachers pigeon hole ideas as, "*too primary* or *too advanced* for my kids." If you are a teacher of elementary grades, some of the transformed activities will appear to be beyond your students. To show you what has been accomplished by elementary teachers and students, consider this—it's a scan of actual student work.

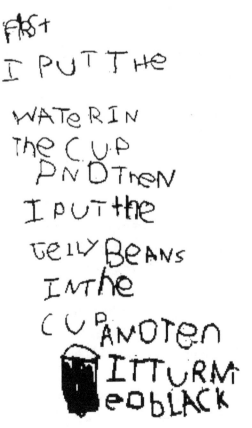

Figure P.1: *Sample of Student Work.*

Obviously, this is from a primary grade student.

We got this sample from Dr. Marilyn Stevens (nee Marquand), who was the Science Coordinator for the San Diego County Office of Education at the time. She had received it as part of a class set of similar papers from one of the teachers working with her in an ongoing professional development program. This scan is one of the most legible of those student papers, but nearly all were of similar quality in the gist of their responses.

When we show this to participants in workshops, we ask two questions.

1. What is the grade level of this student?
2. What is the prompt the teacher used to generate this response?

Most teachers guess *First Grade* for the age and something like, "How did the water turn black?" as the prompt.

Both answers are wrong.

The student was in *Kindergarten*. This assignment was part of a homework task given over spring break.

In twenty years, we've never had a single teacher guess the actual prompt— and we've done this session with close to one thousand teachers over that time span. Dr. Marquand reports this about the prompt:

I always loved that little sheet of paper and the reactions it stirred when folks found the prompt was so open-ended. Teachers always wanted to pigeon hole the answer to fit their own ideas of **correct**. *I probably used that with 100's of teachers and not one got it right. One actually asked if I was afraid of what I'd get if I used a prompt like that. "Uh, no!!!"*

We debated whether or not to put the answer to Question #2 above here, but we want you all to go into our discussion of how you can "…Turn on Student Learning!" with the most open mind possible—*regardless of the age of your students.*

So here is the assignment given to the Kindergarteners over spring break…

"Make up an experiment and write down what happened."

If you are a teacher of high school juniors and seniors, the prompt might not sound difficult. Many of you might think the student example is, at best, minimal. However, for a five- or six-year-old child, *this is very much critical thinking*. And, regardless of the age of the students who received it, the prompt is as open-ended as it gets.

The important piece in this is the work sample. It is *unexpected*. It requires a *shifting of perspective* on student potential and ability to think deeply. The teacher is providing a risk-taking learning opportunity—very much open-ended with neither the teacher nor the student sure what will result. In other words, this teacher was willing to *get out of the way* of her *Kindergarten* students—and look what fantastic results were achieved.[1]

We wish we could tell you that all students will respond to the ideas in this book like our exemplar kindergartener. They won't. But, the vast majority of students **will**—as you implement your interpretation of the steps we suggest in your classes.

The message for **you**, our readers, is: *we realize each of you comes to reading our book for different reasons*. Regardless of your reason for reading it, our intent is to make your journey pleasurable and informative. We want to help you to use what's in this book as an opportunity to do good for you and your students.

Betty Crocker® is not the author of this book. It is not a recipe you can follow step by step and get a perfect award winning "cake" at the end. This is a map of the change process with "GPS coordinates" included.

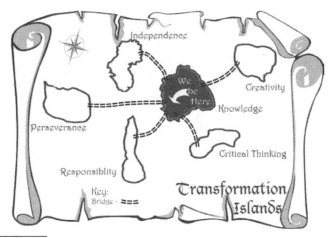

---

1   For another example of teachers who "got out of the way," see Penner et al. in References.

Enough!

Let the *transformation* begin.

Dr. JoAnn Jurchan
Dr. Chuck Downing

ACKNOWLEDGEMENTS

- Linda Morris, Marilyn Marquand, Elena McComas, and Anne Boyer for critical reads, reviews, and endorsements.
- Artists and former high school students of Dr. Downing, Alison Long—main text figures—and Taylor Maggiacomo—methods of transportation in The Analogy.
- Our students and colleagues who provided quotes throughout the text.

WHY YOU SHOULD READ THIS BOOK
AN UNCOMMON FOREWORD

Cast:	**Dr. Bonnie Brunkhorst**, Past President, National Science Teachers Association (NSTA); Professor of Science Education and Professor of Geological Sciences, Emeritus, California State University, San Bernardino.
	Dr. JoAnn Jurchan and *Dr. Chuck Downing*, co-authors.
Dr. Brunkhorst:	I'm glad you asked me to write a Foreword for your book. In my career, I've been a classroom science teacher, a district administrator, and then a university professor. I am also a parent and grandparent. I care deeply about our students and their teachers. What goes on in the students' classroom is what determines what they really learn there, are able to do, and if they develop a love of learning.
Dr. Downing:	I want to thank you for helping us.
Dr. Brunkhorst:	You are welcome. I do have a request.
Dr. Jurchan:	Of course!

Dr. Brunkhorst: Can you give your readers and me your vision for where this book can help lead us? To what kind of classroom learning environment are you pointing?

Dr. Downing: Our vision is to empower teachers and their students to transform classroom environments that constrain learning into environments that cultivate purposeful and reflective creative thinkers.

Dr. Brunkhorst: I really like your goal of *"environments that cultivate purposeful and reflective creative thinkers."* Do you provide a pathway from constrained to effective learning?

Dr Downing: We do provide direction. We consider the *why* and a variety of options on *how* to transform classroom learning environments. The pathway a teacher ultimately chooses must be unique in some way.

Dr. Jurchan: We *can* assist teachers to realize the goal where classrooms are full of students who have the opportunity to learn to their full potential and experience the excitement of learning.

Dr. Brunkhorst: That will be a huge contribution to our students' lives!

Dr. Jurchan: Thank you. We explore classroom conditions and teacher and student practices that cultivate or constrain the learner's ability to achieve effective learning, thus expanding their potential.

Dr. Brunkhorst: Outstanding vision! Now, I know this book is targeted for a variety of people that can influence what students experience in the classroom—teachers (both veterans and early career), administrators at all levels, and parents. Let's assume I entered an elevator with you, saw you holding your book, and asked, "Why should I read your book?" Since you don't know to which of your target audiences I belong, how do you answer that question before I get to my floor?

Dr. Downing: In our book, we give explanations of the *why* and a variety of options on *how* to *transform* classroom environments that *constrain* learning *into* environments that *cultivate* purposeful and reflective creative thinkers.

Dr. Brunkhorst: How do you do that?

Dr. Jurchan: The underlying goal is to change the current "us" versus "them" culture between teachers, administrators, students, and parents into a cohesive "we" where everyone has the same information on what the learning experience can be, especially the students.

Dr. Brunkhorst: I really like your "especially the students" and their teachers.

Dr. Downing: The informed "we" has more potential to implement transforming change as it is based on an agreed upon foundation of principles and practice.

Dr. Jurchan: Is that the vision you're looking for?

Dr. Brunkhorst: I think so. I am impressed with your collaborative approach to making the best learning environments for our students... of all ages. It seems grounded on mutual respect among all that guide our students' learning. It respects the mixed expertise of all, "especially the students" and their teachers. It places the teachers and students at the top of the pyramid. It helps the rest of us not in the classroom to support the professionalism and understandings of the teachers and their students. It empowers the teachers to guide their students' natural curiosity and creativity along productive potentials for each learner.

If we can make the classroom a place where the best learning opportunities are available and expected for our students, in an atmosphere of respect, support, encouragement, and caring, then we know we're making a huge contribution to their lives. Isn't that what we're trying to do?

Many thanks to you for offering a pathway to helping make lives better. I hope readers will be able to share their experiences and those of their students with you.

Dr. Jurchan: And so do we. We'd love to hear from them.

Dr. Downing: In fact, our website, www.engageinthinking.com, has specially designed places for just that type of interaction.

Dr. Jurchan: Our email and snail mail contact information is on the site as well.

Dr, Downing: So, after all this, are you still willing to write that Foreword for us?

Dr. Brunkhorst: Well... I think *we've* "written" *your* Foreword *together*. How's that for modeling "WE"!

Chapter 1

WHY WE WROTE THIS BOOK
WHO CARES? SERIOUSLY...

Chapter Overview - Knowledge Island

You begin your journey with us at the center island, **Knowledge**, from our map of the Transformation Islands. In this chapter, we provide you with our rationale for the book itself, an overview of the process we recommend for you to get the "most" out of your reading, and our list of the Seven Essential Questions you'll be answering as you travel. We end Chapter 1 with some content, providing you with our definition of learning and a statement of our commitment to honor you and your career.

A Quote to Kickstart Your Thinking

> I went to a training on inquiry learning that was eight sessions long over five months. Some time later, I started working on increasing the level of student responsibility for their learning in my classes. It wasn't until I started deciding what changes to implement and implementing

them that I realized I'd learned more about how to do inquiry by deciding and implementing than in all those hours of training.

R.W. - High School Teacher

If you have not read the Preface, please do it now before reading any of the chapters. Information found there sets the tone and provides necessary context for optimal understanding of the rationale for much of the content of this book.

Purpose and Background for this Book

In our combined seventy-four years of teaching, we have witnessed myriad educational movements and trends come and go. Like all other teachers, we have been called upon and held responsible for effectively implementing new policies, programs, curricula, educational approaches, methods, and school structures. Depending on your teaching tenure, you might remember project-based learning, smaller learning communities (school within a school model, for example), the whole language approach, phonics, integrated math and science, or providing academic targets for students during lessons.

Some changes to the educational landscape have proven exciting and were truly transformational in nature. For example, the move away from tracking students by alleged ability levels was transformational. Tracking pigeonholed students—too often for their entire K-12 academic careers. Providing heterogeneous classes opened doors to higher education for thousands of learners.

Of course, some attempted changes have proven to be unsuccessful and ineffective… we'll let you determine which of those changes you remember and in which category they fit.

There is, however, one cornerstone of the educational "building" that has not changed—the indispensable requirement that all students become ready to engage in meaningful and rigorous thinking. The high quality of this type of thinking compels students to be persistent—each one becoming an intellectual risk-taker, competent in the use of learning strategies and methods. Ultimately, students like these are characterized by intrinsic motivation, disciplined minds, and well-developed problem-solving skills—all necessary for "real world" achievement and life-long learning.

Our journey in writing this book has taken us back to the fundamentals of teaching and learning. As we dissected the teaching/learning process, we looked for specific scenarios, recognizable signposts, and GPS coordinate locations along the way. As we found indicators that helped emphasize strategic teacher and student choices and behaviors, two things became clear.

1. When those indicators were intentionally connected in classrooms, they generated outcomes that can be positioned along a continuum of passive to active learning and teacher dependent to student independent learning.
2. The more indicators present, the more active, student-dependent learning was present.

Finally, this book is closely associated with an interactive online interface[2] (**www.engageinthinking.com**) that provides a professional forum for educators at all grade levels and levels of experience[3] to explore the practices and conditions that constrain or cultivate a learner's ability to achieve excellence. Please visit the website often and add your knowledge to the base.

What You Will Find in Each Chapter

Each of the eight chapters in this book is structured similarly. Some more closely align to the model that follows than others, but all have the same components in roughly the same sequence.

All chapters begin with an **Overview** of the chapter's content.

A **Quotation** from a practitioner or student that supports the chapter's key components follows the Overview. Some students were in school at the time of publication of this book. Other students quoted are now successful members of a variety of professions. Some chapters have additional quotes that focus on specific topics.

---

2   See Step #8 in the Recommended Process section that follows in this chapter for one way to interact online.

3   We consider *the teacher* (**you**!) as a student and life-long learner in this process.

A **Discussion** of pertinent educational theories and models is presented. This is the "meat" of the chapter.

Example of Transforming a Common Activity segments provide examples of application of a theory or model. These examples demonstrate one way that you can integrate and use the theory. In most chapters, the Example of Transforming a Common Activity segment starts with a *Common Activity*. This is a prompt of the same type that is common to multiple grade levels and disciplines. Typically, a prompt is presented using context or verbiage for three or four grade levels or disciplines.

Immediately following the *Common Activity* is a *Transformed Activity*. This is a redesign of the common version that improves engagement and rigor in thinking. Commentary on *how to perform the transformation* and *how the redesigned activity improves the level of thinking* is included.

The last component of these sections is a set of *Teacher Notes* for the Transformed Activity. These allow you to implement the lesson immediately, if you desire. You can also use the Commentary and Teacher Notes as "How To Guides" for developing your own activities—our ultimate goal for you.

One or more **"He Said/She Said"** dialogs (or **"She Said/He Said,"** depending on who initiates the dialog) between Dr. Jurchan and Dr. Downing are included. One side of each dialog will emphasize the theory and models; the other will ask clarifying questions or offer alternative verbiage for describing or explaining a particular idea or concept. These are intended to do one of two things.

1. Spark your thinking about the concepts just previously presented.
2. Ask clarifying questions—perhaps similar to those you've been thinking of while reading.

You might have questions that we didn't think of. We encourage you to take advantage of our online discussion board and begin dialogs of your own with us and other practitioners.

Recommended Process

After reading this chapter, your next step is to read **The Analogy**, *Building Boats*, which focuses on teaching, engagement, and learning. The chart that follows **The Analogy** is for you to fill in. Having worked with teachers for many years, we know that some/*many*/**most** of you may choose to "do it your way." That's reality. However, we're convinced that adhering to our recommended process will help you get the most benefit from your experience. In addition, following the recommended procedure will provide a visual record of your progress as you modify your approach to how teaching and learning occurs in your classroom.

So, *step-by-step*, we recommend you complete the following eight steps in order.

1. Finish reading this chapter!
2. Read **The Analogy** that follows this chapter straight through. Do not stop and fill in the chart that follows The Analogy. "Do not pass Go. Do not collect $200."

Table 1.1. *Portion of the Chart for Analogy Analysis*

¶#	Immediately after reading **The Analogy** for the first time.	After reading **The Analogy** and parts/all of the book.
I.	*MIDDLE COLUMN*	*THIRD COLUMN*

3. Fill in the **MIDDLE** column of the chart that follows this chapter with your thoughts and ideas on what each of the characters and situations in **The Analogy** represent in a/your classroom. If you'd prefer, there is a downloadable 8.5" x 11" version on our website.
4. Read through Chapter 2 of the book. Again, don't stop when you have an "Ah, ha!" moment. By continuing to read after you have an idea, instead of stopping and recording anything new on your chart, you force your brain to begin forming a memory path to that idea. This

makes remembering the idea later an easier task. Occasionally, we **will** ask you to make changes to your chart. Yep—right then and there!

5. After you have finished reading each chapter in its entirety without stopping to make any changes, go back to **The Analogy** and the chart. Whether we direct you or not, this is when you record your new thinking. You record your new thinking or clarifying statements to your first thoughts about **The Analogy** in the **THIRD** column.

6. Continue the process in steps 3-5 until you have completed all the chapters in the book and have all three columns in your chart filled in.

 Periodically throughout this book, this direction will appear with a shaded text box of directions. Follow the prompt in each box and keep your responses available for reflection.

7. Go to our website www.engageinthinking.com. Use your code to login to the page /boatbuilding. Enter the discussion on the ideas included in **The Analogy**. Modify your chart answers as you see fit. While you have "our permission" to go to the website after each individual chapter, if you know you'll "look ahead" (and you know if you will!), wait until this step before checking **our ideas**. *This means you shouldn't know what **we** think until after **you've** thought!*

8. After exchanging ideas with your peers and making modifications to your chart answers as you see fit, compare your ideas and answers to those provided with your access code.[4]

Discussion of Educational Theories and Models

What we know about the field of education is that there is not "one right way" to teach or learn. We also know that there are practices and ways of thinking about teaching and learning that are considered "best"—the litmus test most often being levels of student achievement. Teacher education courses and professional development events often focus on the "how to do" or the "how to measure" pieces of those practices—the application and accountability

---

4   Go to our website www.engageinthinking.com. Once there, use your access code to log in. Find the "Analogy Answers" icon and give it a click.

phases. Traditionally absent, except when included in an introductory course to education, is additional study or review of the *purpose* of the educational system—developing and implementing the attributes necessary for effective *learning*. So, it is at this elemental *but indispensable* point we begin our journey.

Seven **Essential Questions** that we address throughout this book are listed in **Figure 1.1**. These are designed to serve as catalysts for reflection, discussion, and meaningful, long-lasting change.

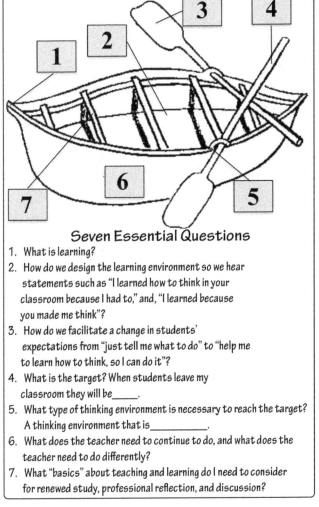

Seven Essential Questions

1. What is learning?
2. How do we design the learning environment so we hear statements such as "I learned how to think in your classroom because I had to," and, "I learned because you made me think"?
3. How do we facilitate a change in students' expectations from "just tell me what to do" to "help me to learn how to think, so I can do it"?
4. What is the target? When students leave my classroom they will be_____.
5. What type of thinking environment is necessary to reach the target? A thinking environment that is_____.
6. What does the teacher need to continue to do, and what does the teacher need to do differently?
7. What "basics" about teaching and learning do I need to consider for renewed study, professional reflection, and discussion?

Figure 1.1: *Essential Questions to Answer.*

Throughout this book you will be generating answers to these.

A Definition of Learning

To say that the question "What is learning?" is broad is an understatement. Volumes have been filled with attempts to provide the definitive answer to that question. Vigorous and impassioned discussions have taken place across the ages generating multiple responses. Issues of culture, power, equity, and equality all influence the answer to the question. Policies, regulations, and legislation have grown out of attempts to manage the then current answer to "What is learning?" Enormous collections of resources in multiple forms have been committed to carrying out a succession of the latest and "best" decisions of how to include what learning encompasses in curricula.

We do not claim to have crafted the best definition of learning. However we offer the following to provide you with a foundation and a glimpse into our perspective on this **Essential Question**.

We define learning as:

- *a social process* requiring appropriate challenge in terms of novelty, complexity, depth, and quantity.
- *a mental process* requiring the development of metacognition—the *monitoring* of understanding, the *awareness* of the need for assistance or correction, and the *ability* to recognize and effectively employ cognitive strategies.
- *a perceptual process* involving active processing and attention to schemata (an organizational or conceptual pattern in the mind) that enables the learner to acquire, process, and organize information for new learning.
- *a collaborative process* requiring support and feedback that are both developmental and context specific and have as their ultimate goal the release of responsibility of the learning *to the student*.

Your students' brains are designed to find meaning through patterns and connections in an environment that acknowledges and respects the emotional and social dimensions of learning. For optimal learning to take place, the influencing factors of emotional safety, appropriate challenge, and self-constructed meaning must be effectively integrated. [**Essential Question #1**]

From Definition to Practice: A Preview

How do we design the learning environment so we hear statements such as "I learned how to think in your classroom because I had to," and, "I learned because you made me think"? [**Essential Question #2**]

And how do we facilitate a change in students' expectations from "just tell me what to do" to "help me to learn how to think, so I can do it"? [**Essential Question #3**]

We accept that learning is developmental—sequential at times and spiraled at others. And, learning is sustained through informed practice. As you engage with us in exploring the implications of our **Essential Questions** and the answers we provide, we are committed to providing you with the following:

- a *procedure* to self-assess on critical components for the intentional and knowledgeable creation of a healthy, vibrant, and exciting classroom environment.
- an *opportunity* for you to hone your skills as a reflective practitioner via both professional self-study and collaborative discourse with colleagues.
- the *respect* to bring forward the experience and expertise you already have and tap into it as you review, refine, and revitalize your craft as an educator.
- a *safe, non-punitive setting* to honestly address the "just think harder" statements, both spoken and unspoken, that may arise in your teaching.
- an *invitation* to correct the erroneous thinking that if teachers only knew more about the content they teach, then student achievement would naturally improve—an idea that indicates a lack of understanding of the complexity of teaching and learning.

"She Said/He Said"[5]

Dr. Jurchan: Do you think our readers will be offended because we provided them with recommendations to follow when reading this book and then expressed concern that they may not do what we have suggested?

Dr. Downing: I doubt it. In my experience, teachers tend to be the worst students—and they usually know that.

Dr. Jurchan: We do sometimes like to do it "our own way," but I think they will do what we have asked.

Dr. Downing: Hopefully most teachers *will* follow our suggested pathway.

Dr. Jurchan: It really will help them understand what we've tried to accomplish with this book.

Dr. Downing: Good point. Should we explain *why* we have a recommended process?

Dr. Jurchan: We did that with the explanation about how it helps them remember what they've processed.

Dr. Downing: There must be other reasons, too.

Dr. Jurchan: Yes, there are.

Dr. Downing: So...

Dr. Jurchan: We probably shouldn't give them a long list of "whys" at this point.

Dr. Downing: Fair enough. But, I'm going to be checking along the way. We can't just expect blind obedience when the book we wrote is all about developing independent thinkers!

Dr. Jurchan: As they follow our recommended process in each chapter, rationale will be developed and more reasons for our suggestions will emerge.

Dr. Downing: Okay. But, I'm still not convinced—Wait a minute! Didn't we promise that each chapter would have at least an *Example of Transforming a Common Activity*?

---

5   In all subsequent "**She Said/He Said**" dialogs, character names will be **Dr. J** and **Dr. D**

Dr. Jurchan: We did—we can't forget that part. It's critical to our promise to connect what we are saying *can and should* be done to *how* it can be accomplished.

Dr. Downing: Well then, they'd best read on.

Example of Transforming a Common Activity

Table 1.2. *List of Learning Tasks*

Analysis	Complex Tasks	Creativity	Curiosity	Engagement
Metacognition	Multiple Tasks	Persistence	Real World Tasks	Synthesis

A list of Learning Tasks culled from current educational reform movements is presented in **Table 1.2.** While this specific list appears in no individual reform movement's official documentation, investigation of those documents reveals these terms, or variations of them, in all of them. As part of this segment of each chapter, these Learning Tasks will be referenced where the concept is represented in the common or transformed activity by **bolding**[6] of the term.

- **Common Social Science Assignment:** *List the main causes of America's Revolutionary War.*
- **Common Language Arts Assignment**: *List the main reasons the romance of Romeo and Juliet was doomed from the start.*
- **Common Science Assignment:** *List the traits of arthropods.*
- **Common Elementary Math Assignment:** *List the main reasons for multiplying instead of adding numbers.*

Commentary: This assignment is completed by having students look through their textbook or by taking notes from a teacher's direct instruction. The student is asked to perform no higher-level thinking. None of the

---

6   See the example in the following paragraph or the "Teacher Notes" on the Transformed Social Science Activity that follows.

Learning Tasks are addressed, with the possible exception of the lowest level of **Engagement**.

> **Example Transformed Social Science Activity**: *List five main causes of America's Revolutionary War. Rank them from most important to least important. Explain why you chose the causes you chose as most important and least important.*

To add another wrinkle to this assignment, consider this alternative modification: *Write a short recruiting speech for a Colonial militia officer as he speaks to potential soldiers about why they should join the American side in the war.* For the other examples in this section, the speech might be to **a)** other characters in the play (Language Arts), **b)** a group of exterminators in training (Science), or **c)** to their classmates persuading them to accept the rationale provided in the recruiting speeches for both functions (Math).

Commentary and Teacher Notes (Social Science task)

For the First Transformation

- Although this assignment begins as the *common* assignment, with the development of a list, the ranking of causes requires **Analysis** by the student. The explanation of the ranking of most important and least important is a form of **Metacognition** as students are required to think about and *express their thinking* in making the ranked list.
- In many corporate job situations, employees are expected to defend suggestions and recommendations they have developed or researched to a supervisor or committee. This modification is a low-level example of a **Real World Task** in that regard.
- If you require the ranked list with justification in the form of a table, it allows you to provide checkpoints during the process and assist students with misconceptions or erroneous ideas.

For the Second Transformation

- Before writing their speech, students must still develop a list, rank the list, and justify their ranking, at least in their own minds—completing all the Learning Tasks as in the first transformation.

- This assignment adds **Creativity** and **Synthesis** to the list of Learning Tasks addressed.
- As desired, the speeches could be presented to the class or to a small group of students.
- To add still another layer to this activity, half the students could write recruiting speeches for the Colonial Militia, and the other half could write speeches for the Tories/Loyalists (Americans who, during the period of the American Revolution, favored the British side).
- If you choose to have both Colonial and Tories/Loyalist speeches, after they are written, form two "expert groups" of each persuasion. Have each expert group select one speech to be delivered to the class. Presentations of the four speeches should alternate the Colonist view and the Loyalist view.
- After all speeches are given, each class member votes for the side (s) he chose to support and explains why that choice was made. Student rationale for supporting their choice should include both pros and cons. Student arguments must be based solely on the information presented in the four speeches.
- This additional layer strengthens **Engagement** by encouraging buy-in to a particular position. It strengthens the **Real World Task**—this is what Americans (should) do in each election. By the end of this alternative to "List the causes of the American Revolutionary War," students will have completed a very **Complex Task**, indeed.

"He Said/She Said"

Dr. D: So I think we've covered all the parts of the chapter as we promised. How about you?

Dr. J: I think we need to reiterate why the terms are bolded in the Transformation section.

Dr. D: Each bolded term refers to where that Learning Task from Table 1.2 is highlighted in the task.

Dr. J: Great. Thanks.

Dr. D: How are we going to end this chapter?

Dr. J: I have an idea.

Dr. D: Be my guest.

Dr. J: [*Best Announcer's Voice*] And now, we would like to take you on a journey... to a kingdom of long ago. Ruled by a benevolent Monarch and inhabited by loving subjects. Our story and your journey begin here and now.

THE ANALOGY
BUILDING BOATS

**An analogy for how your students can
"Engage in Thinking" in your classroom**

Throughout this analogy, the Monarch and the Wise Advisor are referred to as "she" and "he," not because of any implication of gender, but because the English language does not have a gender-free pronoun.

Table A.1: *Learning Goals or Tasks as in Chapter 1*
[These are marked where they occur in The Analogy by: (#)]

1. Analysis	2. Complex Tasks	3. Creativity	4. Curiosity	5. Engagement
6. Metacognition	7. Multiple Tasks	8. Persistence	9. Real World Tasks	10. Synthesis

I. Once upon a time, there was a benevolent Monarch. She loved her subjects and they loved her.

II. The kingdom she ruled was an island. In the distance, other islands could be seen, but only a very few, very strong, very determined subjects ever swam to other islands. When they returned, if asked, the swimmers spoke of exciting new ideas, places, and events. But the long, long swim still kept nearly all of the Monarch's subjects at home on her island kingdom. **(8)**

III.   The Monarch's heart was broken for her people—most isolated and without hope of visiting the neighboring islands to feast, explore, and learn new things. Determined to help them she learned to fly, and built an airplane. Without cost to her subjects, she used her airplane to deliver all who desired to any of the islands.

IV.   Many of her people traveled to different islands, taking what luggage they chose with them. Each island held a different tempting lure for the Monarch (independence, creativity, critical thinking, responsibility, perseverance). However, after visiting an island on the Monarch's airplane, her subjects' description of the experience was almost always identical to the words the Monarch used to describe her encounter with that island—only those subjects who swam to the islands and back seemed to find unique flavors and events to describe.

V.   After a while, however, some of her subjects stopped using the Monarch's free flight service. (**5**) *"It's the same over on other islands as it is here,"* they said. *"We are bored. All we really need is to listen to your descriptions, anyway."*

VI.   Those words puzzled and dismayed the Monarch. She decided to make the trip to the islands take longer, reasoning that personal cost of invested time would increase the value of the reward—after all, she had invested much time and energy in visiting those wonderful places. Using materials from her kingdom, she built bridges to several of the islands. Her subjects could freely traverse the bridges with their luggage in carriages she provided. Nearly all the subjects who had stopped riding the airplane tried the carriages and bridges. Some of the fliers chose to travel over the bridges as well. However, most of the fliers continued to use the free airplane for their travel. (**4**)

VII. The bridge and carriages pleased some of those who were not flying anymore. Many of the non-fliers rode the carriages and enjoyed the ride. But some stopped riding the carriages soon after that service began.

VIII. *"It's still boring,"* they declared.

IX. Perplexed again, the Monarch decided to offer a choice for bridge-users: they could ride in carriages, with their luggage stored safely aboard by porters, or each could walk, pushing a cart with his or her luggage packed in it by the traveler.

X. Once again, some of the non-flying, non-bridge using subjects took the offer. They chatted and sweated as they crossed the bridge. As the Monarch hypothesized, there was something to be said for doing work to get the rewards on the islands at the other end of the bridges. (**8**)

XI. But still some subjects chose not to leave the island, and some of those who were using various methods of transportation also quit using them. The Monarch could not believe what she was seeing! Why didn't all her subjects take advantage of her generous offers?

XII. One day, a Wise Advisor gained audience with the Monarch.

"Your Highness, I fear that many of your subjects have no desire to visit other islands because it has cost them so very little," the Advisor said. "When something costs the recipient nothing, even a gift can become unappreciated." The Wise Advisor went on to reveal a plan to the Monarch.

XIII. Soon thereafter, the number of airplane flights was cut, the number of carriages was decreased, and the number of carts available for luggage was reduced.

XIV. In place of those lost items, there appeared mounds of materials along the coast of the island kingdom. Piles of instruction booklets were stacked beside the materials. Curious, subjects read the booklets and several began to follow the instructions. After some struggles, nearly all who tried discovered they were able to build a cart of their own in which to store their luggage on the trips across the bridges.

XV. Since there were also fewer carriages, some subjects asked if they could ride in another's cart with the luggage. And so some did; but the choices were limited to riding or pushing. And only one person at a time could safely be carried in any cart. Some builder/pushers talked of the great satisfaction they achieved by helping others, while some of the riders spoke glowingly of their benefactors.

XVI. The Monarch was very pleased by the sense of appreciation and feelings of accomplishment her subjects achieved when they provided their own transportation and/or helped others with their travel. She reasoned that with competence, skills, and knowledge obtained through cart building, her subjects might like a completely new challenge. Soon, along with the instructions and materials for building carts, the same items were provided for building boats. To her delight, many chose to build a boat to carry them across the water to the next island. Individually, and in small fleets, boats made the trip with occupants rowing to supply power to their own vessels.

XVII. As her subjects rowed their boats, they began to notice the beauty of the islands and to appreciate the variety of experiences found on the different islands. She heard less and less about the airplane. **(2, 5, 9)**

XVIII. Before long, there were many more boat trips than all other modes of transportation combined. The boat-rowing subjects raved about how proud they were of their boats. They regaled all who would listen with stories about adventures on islands they visited in their boats. They discovered that the same boat could go to many islands, which pleased them immensely.

XIX. As time went on, boat-builders began to modify the instructions on their own. They still made boats, but now the boats did not all look the same. There was a sense of pride in building one's own custom boat. A number of subjects formed groups that made bigger boats in which some *rode* and others *rowed*— some even rotated those jobs during the trips to their island destinations. **(3, 10)**

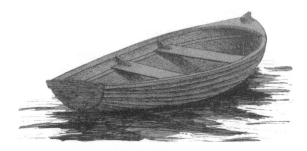

XX. The Wise Advisor again spoke with the Monarch, informing her that **some** subjects were fearful of the boats, but did not want to return to riding in the airplane. He suggested an addition to his plan. The Monarch was pleased and issued an edict, **"You can use another's boat, but eventually, each of you must build a cart or a boat of your own."** (7)

XXI. To insure compliance with her new edict, the Monarch cut the number of free airplane flights to one per month.

XXII. Of course carts and boats had different sets of instructions for their construction, and *most* subjects preferred building carts than building boats or vice versa. In fact, many of the Monarch's subjects had a difficult time choosing what to build. Both the cart and the boat were intriguing, and both were challenging—nearly all seemed eager to try their hand at construction. Small groups were overheard talking about which option to take—they often reconvened after they finished to discuss similarities and differences in the cart-building and boat-building processes.

XXIII. As time passed, she observed that some of her subjects were quite good at building, while others needed more direction to complete the mode of transportation—a few even asked for instructions on how to build a carriage for themselves and others!

XXIV. As more and more boats traveled the waters, swimmers became interested in this method of travel. Some of them were satisfied by the answers to their questions to the boat builders. Other swimmers joined in the boat building process. Since they knew the interisland passages better than the boat builders, many of those swimmers chose to become navigators for the custom boats. This teamwork helped novice sailors avoid treacherous waters and submerged obstacles—and the swimmers gained a new perspective on traveling around the islands. The Monarch observed this and was pleased that both swimmers and builders were cooperating.

XXV. As more time passed, the Monarch realized that now, when her subjects spoke of trips to and experiences on other islands, their words sounded very much different than her words of description. Greatly encouraged by this increased level of interest in travel, the Monarch ordered some instruction booklets be written with much detail and other booklets be left intentionally less specific. Her subjects appreciated having choices of both *what* to build and *how* much guidance they received. Eventually, some asked if they could build their own cart or boat—without instructions! (**1, 2, 5, 6, 8, 9, 10**)

XXVI. As more subjects built and used their own carts or boats to get to the islands, fewer subjects crossed the bridges in the carriages or rode in the free airplane. The Monarch was astonished at this. She grounded the airplane entirely and stopped maintaining the bridges. The Wise Advisor spoke yet another time with the Monarch.

"Your Highness, some subjects require the airplane to reach the islands. Others need the bridge. It is not from sloth that they choose not to use the boats or walk the bridge. For some it is lack of experience. For others it is fear of the unknown. Still other subjects will always need the airplane at least part of the time. It is a necessity for them. For others the bridge is a place of security."

XXVII. The Monarch heeded the Wise Advisor's words. From that time on, there remained five methods to travel from the kingdom to the islands: swimming, airplane, carriage, cart, and boat. The number of subjects using each mode of travel ebbed and flowed.

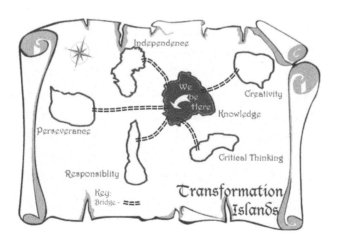

XXVIII. But still, the Monarch was curious as to why so many wanted to build their own transportation rather than use that which she provided for them. She asked her subjects, **"Why do you like the boats better than the airplane?"**

Some answered, *"The boat goes where and when we want it to."* Or, *"We build our boat just the way we like it."* Or, *"The boat is ours, not yours."*

But some answered, *"We don't like the boats. The airplane is faster and less work for us."* Or, *"It's too much like you don't believe in us when we ride the airplane."* Or, *"I like the solid security of the bridge—the other methods of transportation have too many unknowns for me."*

XXIX. When the Wise Advisor met again with the Monarch, the Advisor asked, *"So how do you feel now about your subjects?"*

XXX. "I feel good and bad at the same time," the Monarch admitted. "I am happy for what they are accomplishing, but I am sad that they don't see much need for me any longer. I wish I had your insight and wisdom."

XXXI. *"That is a request I can facilitate,"* the Wise Advisor said with a smile. Taking her hand, the pair rose together into the sky above the Island. As she floated along, she was able to observe her subjects and appreciate their accomplishments and the joy they felt. Yet she knew that she was close enough to help them if they really needed it.

XXXII. And then the Monarch truly understood the words of the Wise Advisor. She saw that her subjects were much better subjects as she allowed them more freedom in how and where they traveled. In fact, she came to realize that the greatest gift she had given them was the freedom to explore and then appreciate their efforts, because they were successful at hard work. The resultant rewards her subjects received were much more valuable to them because of *her* willingness to empower them to do things on their own.

XXXIII. "I think I received more from my subjects than they received from me," she whispered as they came to rest in her castle courtyard.

XXXIV. And the Wise Advisor nodded with understanding.

XXXV. As in all good tales of this sort, to this very day, all the Monarch's subjects travel throughout the islands. Some always use the carts and boats they themselves have built. Some use the carts they have built more than other methods of transportation. Others choose to use the airplane or ride in a carriage across a bridge much more than their own cart or boat. And through all of this time and change, many swimmers still choose to swim to the islands of their choice. (**8**)

XXXVI. All the subjects agreed on one thing. Building their own mode of transportation and using their own handiwork to move about the ***Transformation Islands*** was *"the best thing our Monarch ever did to help us enjoy the other islands."* (**6**)

Jot down any thoughts you might have in this space.

THE ANALOGY
ANALYSIS TOOL

The blank chart that follows is for you. Having worked with teachers for many years, we know that some/many/most of you may choose to "do it your way." That's reality. However, we hope you try our suggested method—we're convinced it will help you get the most benefit from your experience and have a visual record of your progress. (Does this paragraph sound familiar?)

Recommended Process

1. Read **The Analogy** straight through. Do not stop to fill in the chart until you finish the entire analogy.

2. Fill in the **MIDDLE** column with your thoughts and ideas on what each of the characters and situations in **The Analogy** represent in a/ your classroom.

3. Read through Chapter 2 of the book. Again don't stop when you have an "Ah, ha!" moment.

4. Go back to **The Analogy**. Start filling in any modifications to your first thoughts, along with new thoughts about **The Analogy** in the THIRD column.

5. Continue the process in steps 3-4, replacing Chapter 2 with each subsequent chapter, until you have completed the book and have all three columns in the chart filled in.

6. Go to our website www.engageinthinking.com and enter the discussion on the ideas included in **The Analogy**. Modify your chart answers as you see fit.

7. After exchanging ideas with your peers and making any modifications to your chart answers, compare your ideas and answers to those provided with your access code.

Add any notes you might have here

¶#	Immediately after reading **The Analogy** for the first time	After reading **The Analogy** and parts/all of the book
I	Monarch: The teacher.	
II	The Kingdom is a classroom. The other islands in the archipelago represent fundamental destinations for purposeful and reflective creative thinkers.	
III		
IV		

¶ #	Immediately after reading **The Analogy** for the first time	After reading **The Analogy** and parts/all of the book
V		
VI		
VII		
VIII		

¶#	Immediately after reading **The Analogy** for the first time	After reading **The Analogy** and parts/all of the book
IX		
X		
XI		
XII		

¶ #	Immediately after reading **The Analogy** for the first time	After reading **The Analogy** and parts/all of the book
XIII		
XIV		
XV		
XVI		

¶ #	Immediately after reading **The Analogy** for the first time	After reading **The Analogy** and parts/all of the book
XVII		
XVIII		
XIX		
XX		

¶#	Immediately after reading **The Analogy** for the first time	After reading **The Analogy** and parts/all of the book
XXI		
XXII		
XXIII		
XXIV		

¶#	Immediately after reading **The Analogy** for the first time	After reading **The Analogy** and parts/all of the book
XXV		
XXVI		
XXVII		
XXVIII		

¶ #	Immediately after reading **The Analogy** for the first time	After reading **The Analogy** and parts/all of the book
XXIX		
XXX		
XXXI		
XXXII		

#	Immediately after reading **The Analogy** for the first time	After reading **The Analogy** and parts/all of the book
XXXIII		
XXIV		
XXXV		
XXXVI		

Chapter 2

BUT THEY NEED ME, DON'T THEY?
GETTING PAST THE
"SAGE ON THE STAGE" STAGE

Chapter Overview - Independence Island

The first bridge you cross on your journey leads to **Independence Island**. In Chapter 2, you'll explore the various roles of teachers and students in the educational process. With that foundation in place, we offer the Gradual Release of Responsibility Model as an example of how you can help your students move from dependent to independent thinkers and learners in your classroom. We end with a discussion of what characteristics of a learning environment are most conducive to this process.

A Quote to Kickstart Your Thinking

> My initial thoughts on the subject are that when you treat kids with respect and teach them how to question and learn, it's a gift that lasts a lifetime. It teaches them to trust their instincts, to have confidence in their own ability to problem solve. I know that in school, I was most

> excited when I learned something that applied directly to life, when I was engaged in the process and felt a sense of purpose... as with the boat and carriage builders in the story. You are actually learning a myriad of things by doing the tasks... without necessarily realizing that you are "learning". But make no mistake, knowledge is being gained on multiple levels, and often profound levels, that stay with you for a lifetime.
>
> **A.H-D**: *University of California, Irvine*

Discussion of Educational Theories and Models

If you are following our recommendations on how to proceed through this book, you have read through **The Analogy** once and begun to create a mental picture of the characters. You have written an initial explanation and analysis of the meaning of the events described in the narrative by filling in the **MIDDLE** column of the chart. You may also have begun to analyze the dialog between the characters and wondered about the causes, reasons, or motives that are the source for the thoughts and actions of those characters.

For example, initial analysis of the Monarch can take into account the following:

1. duty towards the subjects
2. acceptance of responsibility and guardianship over the subjects
3. choices and actions on behalf of the subjects throughout the story

Your decisions about what each of those includes provide potential points for comparability with and connections to your understanding of teaching and the complementary relationship between teacher and student. Questions regarding the significance of the options provided to the Monarch's subjects and preferences revealed through their choices are to be considered as gauges in the evolution of the teaching and learning process.

In this chapter, we begin to explore:

1. the functions and roles associated with teachers and the establishment of teacher identity

2. the roles associated with students and student identity
3. Gradual Release of Responsibility Model (**GRRM**)
4. scaffolding

As you read this chapter, consider how the content provides insight into the character of the Monarch in **The Analogy**.

First we'll return to two of the Essential Questions to frame the content of this chapter.

- **Essential Question #2**: *How do we design the learning environment so we hear statements such as "I learned how to think in your classroom because I had to," and, "I learned because you made me think"?*
- **Essential Question #3**: *How do we facilitate a change in students' expectations from "just tell me what to do" to "help me to learn how to think, so I can do it"?*

Teacher Roles

If someone were to ask: "How do you define *teacher*?" **Or**, "What distinguishes a teacher's identity from other professionals involved with education?" What would you say?

 Write down your definition of *teacher* and what you feel distinguishes a teacher's identity from other professionals involved with education. Keep this handy!

As teachers, we take on many roles as we carry out our primary function of assisting students to learn. A dictionary definition of "teacher" includes the impartation of knowledge and design of situations that provide a learning environment where students **can** and **will** learn.[7]

The roles we take on reflect more than professional expectations within an historical context—they also represent culture, community, and social/interpersonal relationships. Found at the core of each role, though, is the heart of the teacher—the reason for entering the profession. This "heart" includes

---

7   We'll talk more about the "will" of learning in Chapter 3.

the commitment to "do good," to help, to nurture, to challenge for growth, and to be resolute in finding ways to make content come alive and cultivate students who are enthralled with learning. See **Figure 2.1**.

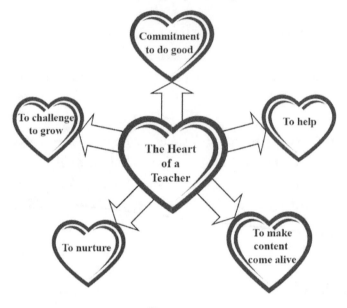

Figure 2.1. *The Heart of a Teacher.*

Harden and Crosby (2000) list six general categories and their associated subcategories for the roles of the teacher. See **Table 2.1**.

Table 2.1: *Teacher Roles and Categories*

Teacher Roles: General categories	Teacher Roles: Subcategories
1. Information provider	Lecturer; Clinical or practical teacher
2. Role model	On-the-job role model; Role model as teacher
3. Facilitator	Learning facilitator; Mentor
4. Assessor	Student assessor; Curriculum assessor
5. Planner	Curriculum planner; Course planner
6. Resource developer	Resource material creator; Study guide producer

Modified from Harden and Crosby (2000).

H. Douglas Brown (Brown 1994; 2007) describes the main roles that a teacher takes on. As you read down the list, these suggested roles become increasingly more favorable to creating and sustaining an interactive learning environment. While Brown's focus is second language teaching and learning, the role descriptions are not constrained by who or what is being taught. See **Table 2.2**.

Table 2.2: *Suggested Roles of Teachers*

Teacher Role	Description of Role
1. Controller	Regulates all that occurs in the classroom—pedagogy, organization, types and conditions for interactions. There is maximum regulation/planning/scripting and minimum spontaneity/unrehearsed interactions.
2. Director	Responsible for an efficient and effective educational process to prepare students for real-life interactions. "Keep the process flowing smoothly and efficiently" (Brown 1994, 161).
3. Manager	Develops overall structure of learning environment and learning opportunities such as instructional planning, pacing of learning activities, goals/objectives, on-going evaluation and feedback. Welcomes individual strengths and expertise to be used and infused in the setting.
4. Facilitator	Described as "a less directive role." Requires a stepping back or down from the directive or managerial roles and level of control. Students "…with your guidance and gentle prodding here than there, find their own pathways to success" (Brown 1994, 161). Intrinsic motivation is at the forefront.
5. Resource	Least directive. Student steps forward with needs and choices.

Source: Brown (1994; 2007).

There is overlap in the roles listed above. Roles are not mutually exclusive. Each role has constructive or beneficial attributes as well as unproductive attributes. Teachers assume all roles at different times and in varied combinations. As the science of teaching and the art of teaching interact, the goal is balance between the roles that is sustained through accurate information about the "who, what, when, where, why, and how" of schooling.

Breen and Candlin (1980) organize the variety of roles that you assume as a teacher in three main categories: teacher as facilitator, teacher as participant, and teacher as researcher and learner.

As facilitator, you oversee and assist in the communication process that occurs between you and your students and your students and the content/learning activities you provide them. You organize resources, act as a resource, and participate in the learning process as both guide and collaborator. Finally, the knowledge and professional skills and abilities developed and refined through experience, observation, and study give rise to your role of teacher as researcher and learner. These role descriptions point to the reciprocal and complementary relationships that can exist between you and your students. They also point to the fluid nature of the learning process. As one teaches, one also learns—the lines between the roles become blurred.

The above lists of teacher roles are not exhaustive. Review the lists, taking time to consider the attributes and responsibilities of each.

What roles are consistent with your experiences?

How would you rate the roles in terms of importance and practicality?

 Write down your answers to the above questions. Add a reflective comment about where you are already doing well and where you see yourself with room for improvement.

The answers to those questions are meaningful. They reveal your beliefs, attitudes, perceptions, and viewpoints that help to develop your teacher identity. In addition, they also shed light on your beliefs, attitudes and perceptions on what you perceive as the roles of your students—our next stop in this chapter.

Student Roles

The words student and learner are synonymous, but to avoid confusion for the following section, we will use the word "student" to refer to one who is under the professional responsibility of a teacher. If you look at dictionary entries for the word "student," the following characteristics are included:

- person studying
- knowledgeable or interested person—somebody who has studied or takes much interest in a particular subject
- person formally engaged in learning
- person who studies, investigates, examines thoughtfully
- attentive and systematic observer
- person actively learning
- someone who goes to school

Which bullet point from the list did you place at the forefront of your thinking? How does your personal definition of "teacher" help to shape your definition of "student"? Is how you rated the teacher roles in terms of importance and practicality evident in your definition? As you read the definitions, what students came to mind as exemplars?

 Write down your ideal definition of "student." Refer to that definition as you read through the rest of this chapter.

The symbolic image or portrayal of "student" is influenced by a fundamental belief of what students come to the educational "table" with—this by default influences the roles students take on and how they engage with teachers in the learning process. Imagine traveling back to the time of Aristotle to study his concept as to how the mind works and learning takes place. The comparison of the mind to a blank writing tablet first appears in the 4th century B.C. and is the precursor to the expression "tabula rasa,"[8] which dates to the 1500's.

---

8   A tabula rasa was a scraped wax tablet that became blank or erased when the wax was heated and then smoothed.

In the 17th century, John Locke postulated that the mind, in its primary state, is a tabula rasa, a blank piece of paper, or an "empty cabinet." The "filling" of the cabinet is a result of experiences. According to Locke, all reason and knowledge is shaped by experience with reflections and sensations being the only sources of ideas. It is significant that education—an appropriate academic curriculum—was one of the three methods Locke suggested as appropriate for filling this cabinet of the mind (Locke 1690; 1693).

The metaphor of the mind as a tabula rasa was altered and accepted over time. It became, and still is, considered an outdated and ill-informed understanding of the inherent features or facets of the mind and how learning proceeds.[9] The negative connotation of the term tabula rasa was a reaction to the "blank slate" and "empty cabinet" concepts of student while the teacher became the sole "writing implement" or "source of filling" in the model.

The role/identity of the student was to be filled and the role/identity of the teacher was to do the filling. The educational process was essentially to move things in one direction—a single path from teacher to student. Harden and Crosby (2000) and Brown's (2007) teacher role categories of information provider, controller, and director are predominant in that model. The role of the student was to become adept at receiving and replicating the teacher-transmitted interpretation of the world.

"He Said/She Said"

> **Dr. D: Whoa! This is pretty harsh!**
> **Dr. J: Well, let's think about this for a minute... Educational decisions were made based on knowledge of the times, beliefs and attitudes about how learning takes place, and what was considered most effective for academic achievement.**

---

9 Authors' Note: We must avoid complacency and over-confidence in our 21st century understanding of the teaching and learning process. With advances in research about how the brain works and how teaching with the brain in mind is actualized, our current beliefs and practices will become outdated and ill informed. But until then, we will persevere in our study and scrutiny of the conditions and processes that are considered optimal for learning.

> **Dr. D:** Be real. It's been over three hundred years since Locke, and some teachers still teach using the tabula rasa model. What hope is there?
>
> **Dr. J:** There are always those who trail blaze. Advances in brain research focused on the process of learning, changes in teacher preparation programs, and professional development on topics from learning preferences, differentiated instruction, and emotional intelligence are exciting and encouraging!
>
> **Dr. D:** And we're hoping that this book is a catalyst for more trail blazing.

Countering the notion that students are nothing more than *receivers* and *replicators* is *constructivism*. Constructivist theory proposes knowledge is constructed when interacting with and influenced by existing information. Descriptions of constructivism stress that students do not start as "blank slates" or empty vessels. Neither do they wait for information to be poured into them. Instead, the role of student is to bring his/her whole self to the learning experience. Social, cultural, experiential, and intellectual elements all interact while learning occurs. The role of the student in a constructivist model is to be an active, engaged, collaborative, and self-

Table 2.3. *Generalized Roles Undertaken by Students and Characteristics of Those Roles*

Student Roles	Characteristics
Receiver	I'll wait for you to give it to me.
Co-Constructor of meaning—sense-making	Can we think/do this together?
Independent inquirer/initiator	I am interested in knowing/trying more, and I will act.
Deliverer	I understand—let me tell/show someone else.
Resource	I am competent in this area. I'll be here if you need me.

motivated constructor of knowledge—ultimately responsible for his/her own learning.

As with teacher roles, there are nuances and amalgamations in student roles—no role is pure. Student roles change with changes in circumstances, experiences, and habits or routines in learning environments.

Generalized roles and characteristics for students are listed in **Table 2.3**.

When reviewing the sets of roles for both students and teachers, it becomes evident that creating an effective teaching and learning environment includes three essential components:

1. acknowledging the various roles for both teacher and student
2. understanding of why and when to employ or emphasize the various roles
3. choosing a model or method that contributes to optimizing the mutual efforts of teacher and student, the instructional decisions, and potential for achieving learning goals

Gradual Release of Responsibility Model

First developed by Pearson and Gallagher (1983), the Gradual Release of Responsibility Model (GRRM) is a widely recognized and well-respected research-based instructional model. GRRM provides a basic blueprint to follow that takes into account the shifting roles of *teacher and student* and the essential and gradual shifts in responsibility for learning *from teacher to student*. According to GRRM, the factors of control and regulation must be exchanged *between you and your students*. You must provide learning opportunities with intentional and measured levels and forms of support.

When viewed from the student perspective, the Gradual Release of Responsibility Model looks like **Figure 2.3**.

The "Partner With Me" element consists of two categories: *You take the lead* and *I'll take the lead*. When you *invite* a student to a partnership, you act as guide and collaborator in the learning experience with the goal being increased competence for independent achievement. To effectively implement the Gradual Release of Responsibility Model, you must develop the awareness

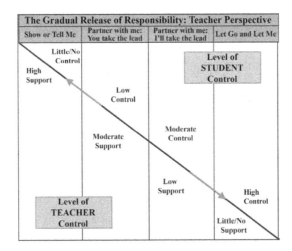

Figure 2.2. *Teacher View of the Gradual Release of Responsibility Model* (Source: Pearson and Gallagher 1983).

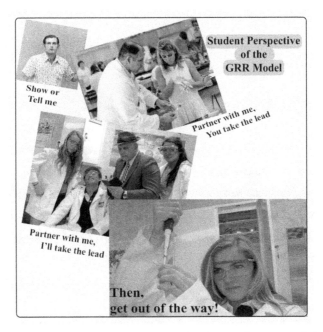

Figure 2.3. *Student View of the Gradual Release of Responsibility Model.* *Show or Tell Me* is Dr. Downing, rookie teacher, in 1973. Remaining photos are Dr. Downing and his students preparing for and working with DNA "evidence" for *Detective* Radtke (Dr. Downing) many years later.

and competence of knowing when to guide, at what pace to progress, how much to guide, and when to let go.

When a student invites you (partner with me, I'll take the lead), you assume the role of scaffold erector. Cues from the student direct what scaffolding or temporary "helps" are needed in order to move the learner closer towards competence and independent achievement. Your expertise and experience come into play as the scaffolds need to be strong enough, stable enough, and in the right location to do the job.

In building construction, adjustments are made to the scaffolding based on what has been completed and what is yet to be built. In GRRM, you do the same thing—adjust the scaffolding. Adjustments are based on knowledge of content, anticipated areas of difficulty, appropriate pedagogy for your student populations, and frequent, formative comprehension checks (Wood, Bruner & Ross 1976). Scaffolding is taken down once the structure is completed. It is superfluous—its purpose is "outlived." *Your responsibility is also to take down the scaffolding when it's no longer needed.* The goal is always the development of learner competence, personal responsibility, and accomplished independent practice and learning.

But They Need Me, Don't They?

Let's review the Essential Questions that provide context for this chapter.

- **Essential Question #2:** *How do we design the learning environment so we hear statements such as "I learned how to think in your classroom because I had to" and, "I learned because you made me think"?*
- **Essential Question #3:** *How do we facilitate a change in students' expectations from "just tell me what to do" to "help me to learn how to think, so I can do it"?*

Both questions emphasize the design of an effective learning environment where students want to think for themselves and insist on taking the reins for their own learning. The questions also acknowledge the critical role that **you** play in providing, guiding, supporting, and then "freeing" your students to become purposeful and effective creative thinkers.

Your students need you. You are the instructional leader in your classroom—
you are trained and certified or credentialed. *You* were hired into a profession
that insists on effective instruction and achievement results. *Your challenge* is to
know when to lead explicitly or directly, when to join/cooperate/collaborate,
and when to step back and observe.

Keep the goal in mind. You want students who

- are independent learners with an enthusiasm for learning
- are engaged "in" learning
- understand, through experience, that learning is work
- have mastered content, developed functional and constructive
  cognitive, social, and emotional skills
- possess the ability to successfully synchronize all these attributes for
  achievement and success

This is a formidable challenge. But achieving the goal (students who…) is
possible when you realize that the goal above is your target!

Essential Question #4: *What is the target?*

 Write down your answer to **Essential Question #4** by completing
this statement. When students leave my classroom they will be
_____. An answer of "independent learners" is not enough.
Be sure to include specific qualifiers and characteristics of
your students. Don't lose this answer. You will be adding to,
subtracting from, and revising it periodically through the rest of
this book.

Teaching and learning is a dynamic and reciprocal process. For effective
instruction and engaged learning to occur, the roles assumed by you and your
students and the subsequent levels of responsibility for the learning must shift
at appropriate times. We encourage *you* to look at instructional possibilities
in different ways while *your students* take personal responsibility for using the
learning opportunities you provide—by learning and practicing the various
roles of a student.

Example of Transforming an Activity

- **Common Language Arts Assignment**: *Use a separate sheet of paper to answer the following questions (instead of taking notes) on the cultural and historical background of the novel <insert title here> in class on the Powerpoint presentation.* (This assignment falls into the "Show or Tell Me" portion of Figures 2.2 and 2.3.)

- **Common Social Science Assignment**: *Use a separate sheet of paper to answer the following questions (instead of taking notes) on the socio-economic factors leading to the French Revolution in class on the Powerpoint presentation.*

- **Common Elementary Science Assignment**: *Use a separate sheet of paper to answer the following questions for a Trade Book. Read the book, <insert name>. Write down one fact from each page about <the topic>.* (The posters described below would illustrate animal or plant structure, the environment in which they function or live, the life cycle of the plant or animal, and how the plant or animal reproduces.)

- **Common Math Assignment**: *Use a separate sheet of paper to answer the following questions: What formulas do you use to calculate perimeter and area of a rectangle and a triangle? What formulas do you use to calculate the circumference and area of a circle? What formulas do you use to calculate the volume of a cylinder and a cube?* (The posters described below would each include an illustration of an architectural structure that contains all of the required shapes listed in the questions.)

Commentary: Good teachers in all disciplines attempt to help students understand material in context. Literature is frequently a reflection of the time and place in which it was written. Without providing background on major historical events, social mores, political intrigues, etc., students of today miss many nuances of period pieces.

Use of a whole class presentation of background material by the teacher is a common method of providing students with context. In this *Common* assignment, the teacher tells all necessary information. Students act as scribes— minimal **Engagement** at best.

We prefer the following assignment, which we think involves high levels of **Engagement** and **Synthesis**. Not only that, but it will work in any subject area in which there are clearly defined subsets or divisions of the concept or topic.

Example of a Transformed Activity

Walking Around a Novel
(Modified from an activity by Jennifer Hsueh)

Description: Before starting a new novel, place ten posters around the classroom that provide facts and information about the book's background.

Steps:

1. Prepare ten movie-sized posters that include facts about the story's setting, time period, and author.
2. Each poster should have pictures and a one to three paragraph blurb about one portion of the background. For example: "The Jazz Age" - "Scott Fitzgerald's life" - "Prohibition."
3. Laminate the posters and space them around the classroom. Use walls, countertops, table/desktops—any adequately sized area will work. Allow ample space around the poster for six to eight students to stand or sit.
4. Prepare five to six questions for each poster that students have to answer.
5. Divide the students into groups of three to four depending on how large your class is. For a class of 40, four per group usually works well.
6. Allow time before the walkaround for explanation of the event.
7. Provide five minutes per poster for students to read and answer questions on the poster's content. Set an alarm so that students have to move onto the next poster when the allotted time is up.
8. When the activity is finished, you could quiz them on the key points from each poster.

Teacher Notes

From Ms. Hsueh: I saw and used this activity during student teaching and found it really useful to get students up and moving. It's a fun way for students to learn without just sitting and reading which tends to happen in English class. I like this activity because it is easily adaptable for many grade levels and it gets students to work together. I used it for an 11th grade American literature class and allowed the students to choose their own groups. This activity works best for books that take place in a time period different from ours. I would definitely use this activity again because the kids seemed to enjoy it and nearly all of them participated.

As written, this *Transformation* of the *Common* assignment is at the *Partner with me, You take the lead* level of Figures 2.2 and 2.3. To raise the level of student control further, moving them to the *Partner with me, I'll take the lead level*, each student group could be responsible for all or part of one poster. You provide the topics and key questions; students do the information search and presentation of that information in their poster. Have groups submit their "information" before they make the poster so you can verify, edit, add, delete (or require students to do those) before the final poster production. (**Creativity** and **Engagement**)

- Unless you have a block schedule, we recommend splitting this assignment over two days, allowing about two-thirds of the class period for Day One and half the period on Day Two.
- Day one: Allow students the freedom to design their posters in any creative way they desire. Again you may choose to hold the "veto power" over a design, if you wish. Groups should post the questions randomly on the poster with the information arranged in a non-linear fashion—by doing that, students have to look at the whole poster to find both information and questions.
- Day two: Provide the questions for each poster on separate papers (one per group).

- Have students number from 1→ "however many questions you have" on a piece of notebook paper. Require all students in the group to rotate writing answers. Do not allow any student to write the answer to more than two consecutive questions. (**Real World Tasks**)
- After fifteen minutes of this second day, student groups could post the answers (checked by you previously) to their key questions in multiple locations around the room. Have groups check answers on which they cannot come to consensus.
- Allow five to ten minutes on the second day for groups to review answers to the key questions. After a review period, collect the question sheets and the group answer sheets.
- Assessment: Select one question from each poster and generate a quiz from those questions. Give the quiz as INDIVDUAL closure on the second day. Since you have more than one question per poster, you can give "customized quizzes" for each period. You might Trade-and-Grade those before the end of the period to reinforce the correct answers.
- Review: You might offer three or four stations that are "repeats" or "catch up" stations where groups or individuals can review previous questions and answers or complete the assignment.

"She Said/He Said"

Dr. J: This chapter presents quite a challenge.

Dr. D: It does indeed. Perhaps if we refocused attention on The Analogy, it might help.

Dr. J: Yes! That will provide a scaffold for our readers as they restructure their existing knowledge with their new learning.

Dr. D: So... how do they do that?

Dr. J: They can find places in The Analogy where specific topics from the chapter are illustrated or represented. For example, they can look for different teacher roles or student roles. They can look for examples of pieces of the Gradual Release of Responsibility Model.

Dr. D: Okay. That's an excellent starting point. But, after reviewing, I think they should update the chart by adding the specific points from this chapter where they see them being demonstrated in The Analogy.

Dr. J: Yes. The review is important but actually writing down their thoughts is critical. It's the revising process that strengthens metacognition—you know, thinking about your thinking.

Dr. D: We just told them again to follow the recommended process for reading this book.

Dr. J: Yes, but I think we said it in a nice way.

Dr. D: So, bottom line: Don't skip steps in the process... Revise!

Dr. J: Yes. Complete the entire recommended reading process before moving on to the next steps.

Dr. D: Enough dialog. We need to let them get to work.

Dr. J: I agree. See you in Chapter 3.

References for Chapter 2

Breen, Michael P., and Christopher N. Candlin. 1980. "The Essentials of a Communicative Curriculum in Language Teaching." *Applied Linguistics* 1 (2): 89-112.

Brown, H. Douglas. 1994. *Teaching by Principles: An Interactive Approach to Language Pedagogy.* Upper Saddle River, New Jersey: Prentice Hall Regents.

_____. 2007. *Teaching by Principles: An Interactive Approach to Language Pedagogy.* 3rd ed. Pearson Education, Inc.

Harden, R.M., and Joy Crosby. 2000. "The Good Teacher is More Than a Lecturer: The Twelve Roles of the Teacher." *AMEE Guide* 22: 334-347. Accessed July 5, 2013. doi:10.1080/014215900409429.

Locke, John. 1690. *An Essay Concerning Human Understanding.* Digireads. com, 2008.

_____. *Some Thoughts Concerning Education: And, of the Conduct of the Understanding,* edited by Ruth W. Grant and Nathan Tarcov. Indianapolis, Indiana: Hackett Publishing 1996.

Pearson, P. David., and Margaret C. Gallagher. 1983. "The Instruction of Reading Comprehension." *Contemporary Educational Psychology* 8: 317–345.

Wood, David, Jerome S. Bruner, and Gail Ross. 1976. "The Role of Tutoring in Problem Solving." *Journal of Child Psychology and Psychiatry* 17(2): 89–100.

Chapter 3

WHAT DO I HAVE TO DO...
STAND ON MY HEAD AND SPIN
TO GET THEM MOTIVATED?
ACCEPTING THAT <u>YOU</u> CAN'T
MOTIVATE ANYONE LONG TERM

Chapter Overview—Creativity Island

Your next bridge leads to **Creativity Island**. On this island, and therefore in this chapter, you'll be looking at: 1) how you can help your students to be self-motivators so they want to take on the creative process of learning; 2) the importance of motivational principles and models in this process; 3) and because we are on Creativity Island, you get a chance to figure out what skateboarding has to do with any of this.

A Quote to Kickstart Your Thinking

> I came into this class hating science. I had always hated science, I believed that I was bad at it, and I had already decided that I would not do well in Biology. However, as the weeks went on, I realized that I was actually quite interested in what I was learning. I began to enjoy the reading and the assignments. After scoring well on a few assessments, I became motivated to learn this subject that I had once abhorred so passionately. I did well in my freshman Biology class because I was interested in the material—because I WANTED [authors' emphasis] to learn. Biology has since become one of my favorite subjects, and I hope to study it further in college.
>
> **KSF**: High School Student

Motivation Research

In Chapter 2, we asked you to begin considering **Essential Question #4**: *What is the target? When students leave my classroom they will be_____.*

We considered the goal of creating a learning environment that propels students forward towards competence as:

- independent learners who are enthusiastic and engaged in learning
- learners who not only understand that learning is "work" (more on that in Chapter 4) but who make choices and act in ways that result in goal attainment
- learners who take responsibility over their learning and achieve through mastery of content
- learners who develop appropriate skills and competencies

Is that all?

Well, no... that and grading, supervising, tutoring, conferencing for starters. Oh, and accomplish it all in approximately 180 days. Do you feel like the scales have tipped measurably towards *teacher responsibility*? Let's consider what can be done to "even up" the responsibilities between you and your students a bit more. We'll start with your students and the influencing factor of motivation.

 Jot down your initial thoughts and feelings about *motivation* and *learning*. Don't censor yourself.

At some point in our teaching careers, we've probably all had the following thoughts:

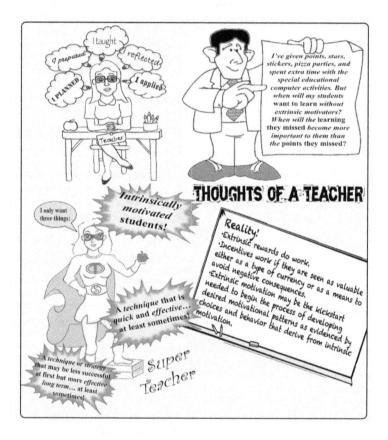

Figure 3.1. *Summary of Teacher Thoughts on Motivation.*

Perhaps the questions we need to ask are: "Do students care about *learning*?" and "When do students care about *learning*?"

Write a *yes* or *no* answer with an explanation to each question. What supporting evidence from your teaching experience and/or observation of teaching and learning environments do you have for either "yes" or "no" answers?

- Did your answers include caveats for degrees of rewards and/or negative consequences?
- Did your answers include differentiating between students whose interests align with or are contrary to the learning experience?
- Where can we find the definitive answer to these **STOP!** questions?

This shouldn't surprise you, but there is no *one* answer. There aren't even just *a few* easy answers. When we talk about what motivates humans and how motivation connects to learning in the classroom, the conversation is broad— both practically and theoretically.

In *Motivating Humans: Goals, Emotions, and Personal Agency Beliefs,*[10] Martin Ford (1992) provides an outline of thirty-two different theories that address human motivation and the evolving conceptual understandings of human development and how humans function. If you just felt your pulse spike, or you just winced involuntarily at the thought of plowing through thirty-two theories on anything, inhale... exhale. Put your mind at ease. We'll look at motivation theory from a few different vantage points and then provide you with a graphic that summarizes key principles of an integrative theory of motivation. Don't forgo reading the remainder of the chapter and just skip to the graphic (**Figure 3.2**). Please keep on reading; you *will* miss essential background information if you skip ahead.[11]

To help motivate *you*, let's jump right into something with very practical applications.

Marge Scherer (2002) in an article titled "Do Students Care About Learning?" reports a conversation with Mihaly Csikszentmihalyi, [Me-high Cheek-sent-me-hi-ee], a renowned researcher and theorist on motivation,

---

10 If you want an in-depth study of motivation theory, this is an excellent resource book.
11 Table based on a synthesis of Martin Ford

creativity, and positive psychology.[12] Csikszentmihalyi recounts a longitudinal study with one thousand students in 6th, 8th, 10th, and 12th grades. Questionnaires, interviews, and programmable pagers were used to document the self-reporting of activities and accompanying thoughts and feelings. The pagers were activated 8 times a day for one week. When the pager went off, the students would journal where they were, what they were doing, what they were thinking, their level of concentration, and how creative and happy they felt about what they were doing when the pager went off. Additionally, the students reported whether or not the activity felt more like work, play, both, or neither. Approximately 30,000 reports were collected over the course of the initial and follow-up studies (Csikszentmihalyi and Schneider 2000). Key Findings from those studies are summarized in **Figure 3.2**.

Ten percent of the activities were reported to be **both** work and play. These appear to contain an ideal mixture of work, challenge, competence, and enjoyment—attributes fueled by goals that are perceived as attainable and valuable.

 Go back to **The Analogy** if necessary to answer this question: Where in **The Analogy** do you find evidence of the Subjects interpreting what they are doing as part of the "The 10%" referenced in **Figure 3.2**? Explain your reasoning.

Two questions must now be asked:

1. What is it about the combination of *work* and *play* that leads to accomplishment or success?
2. What keeps someone moving forward in spite of the obstacles that arise?

---

12   Optimal Experience Theory and Flow – Begin a study of Mihaly Csikzentmihalyis' influential work by reading *Flow: The Psychology of Optimal Experience*. New York: Harper Perennial Modern Classics.

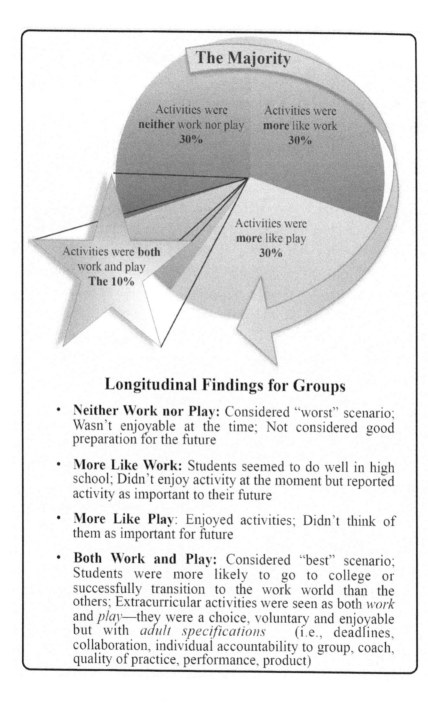

The Majority

Activities were
neither work nor play
30%

Activities were
more like work
30%

Activities were
more like play
30%

Activities were **both**
work and play
The 10%

Longitudinal Findings for Groups

- **Neither Work nor Play:** Considered "worst" scenario; Wasn't enjoyable at the time; Not considered good preparation for the future

- **More Like Work:** Students seemed to do well in high school; Didn't enjoy activity at the moment but reported activity as important to their future

- **More Like Play**: Enjoyed activities; Didn't think of them as important for future

- **Both Work and Play:** Considered "best" scenario; Students were more likely to go to college or successfully transition to the work world than the others; Extracurricular activities were seen as both *work* and *play*—they were a choice, voluntary and enjoyable but with *adult specifications* (i.e., deadlines, collaboration, individual accountability to group, coach, quality of practice, performance, product)

Figure 3.2. *Summary of Students' Responses in Initial and Follow-up Studies.* (Csikszentmihalyi and Schneider 2000).

You, or someone you know, can spend hours practicing a specific skill or developing a talent. The concentration is so complete/intense that you get *lost* in the activity. It does at times look and feel like work, and *hard* work, but that doesn't stop the process because the activity is perceived as *both work and play*. If you were learning how to play a guitar, you would play the same chord over and over again until your fingers were so sore you couldn't go on. This probably seems like too much work to an outsider. But, the next day you're back at it again.

The level of confidence builds throughout the learning process as competence in playing the guitar is developed. Enjoyment comes as a part of the learning when the chord actually sounds like it should. At that point, the work/play scale tilts to the "play" side. There's an inner spark that keeps you practicing. You begin to fantasize of performing as your confidence builds. Time goes by quickly—your attention is solely focused on the task at hand.

At the end of it all, whether as an epiphany or just a growing realization, the *process* is reward enough. Your fantasies, once critical to the journey, are no longer needed motivators.

Csikszentmihalyi identifies this experience as *flow:*

[F]low describes the spontaneous, effortless experience you achieve when you have a close match between a high level of challenge and the skills you need to meet the challenge

(Scherer 2002, 14).

The intrinsic reward system, the close match of the challenge and your skill set, serves as the fuel to continue the hard work, growth, and development. You, as a guitar player, want to learn to play an entire song or compose a song of your own.

"He Said/She Said"

Dr. D: This may be out of sequence, but these ideas have me thinking.

Dr. J: Sometimes a dangerous thing, but I'm listening.

Dr. D: Yeah, I know. Anyway, I think that success by itself is motivating to do other stuff well. When a teacher plans and directs students into successful learning experiences, it lessens the need for extrinsic motivators.

Dr. J: I agree with both your comment and conclusion. Doing well at something is self-motivating. In addition, the concept of success as a motivator works in all classrooms.

Dr. D: That's also a solid reason to differentiate instruction/assignments regardless of your class composition. When you provide a variety of assignment types in the course of a unit of instruction, students who do well on one type of assignment are more willing to put forth effort on another type as a result.

Dr. J: Correct. Different types of assignments provide differing levels of challenge to different students. But, each assignment needs to include a bit of mystery, an unknown, a different perspective.

Dr. D: Hmmm. So, it's not just the type of assignment or instruction that's motivational. Seems to me that if you know you're going to be successful every time, there's no need to put forth much effort.

Dr. J: Yes! It's like someone who plays a game and wins every single time. There is little or no motivation to continue putting forth effort because the outcome is a certainty– the thrill part of the challenge is missing.

Dr. D: What if the game player chose a different game?

Dr. J: The success the player experienced in one game often provides the motivation to put forth the effort required to learn and win at another game.

Dr. D: So, if a student is a good artist, she might be more willing to tackle an assignment in another discipline that intimidated her before her success.

Dr. J: Yes, partly. Hopefully, the success factor, which is competence, would transfer to another learning experience.

The artist has internalized, "I am successful, and I am willing to take on another challenge." The artist probably would also explore new media in art in order to raise the level of difficulty by providing a hurdle she is confident she can clear because of past success. However, additional effort will be required.

Dr. D: Whoa! That's a mouthful! Let me see if I am tracking. If we go back to The Analogy, one reason the subjects stopped using the airplane, and other transportation provided by the Monarch, was that the amount of effort (the motivation) required was minimal. But the Subjects were willing to try other modes of transportation because they knew there were still additional places to go, and they had already had success in one mode of transportation.

Dr. J: That's part of it. The other piece reminds me of the *Twilight Zone* episode where a gambler awakens in a city where he wins every bet. At first he is ecstatic, and he thinks he's in heaven. As the program progresses, the gambler becomes less and less motivated to even place a bet. Finally, he complains to someone about how much different heaven is than he thought it would be. In true *TZ* fashion, just before Rod Serling's voice over, the gambler hears from what he takes to be an angel, "I'm terribly sorry. I thought you were aware. This isn't heaven."

Dr. D: Oh, I get it. The gambler is like the game player. Always winning isn't of itself continually motivating. I guess it's time to "return to our regularly scheduled programming."

Dr. J: What?

Dr. D: Sorry. The *Twilight Zone* reference shoved me into a television moment.

We've provided a glimpse into the prolific work of one influential theorist in the field of human motivation and development. Here are a few key thoughts for you to take away

- intrinsic motivation requires clear and definite personal goals in the context of an optimally challenging task or activity
- a sense of personal control and effectiveness is necessary
- feedback is essential—immediate feedback is ideal (consider our budding guitar player—the sound of the chord provides *immediate* feedback)

Reaching "The Majority"

If "The 10%" in **Figure 3.2** were "*The 90%*," your life as a teacher would be blissful. But, it's not. So, let's tackle the topic of motivation and learning from another vantage point. Phillip Venditti (2001) proposes that the effectiveness of motivational efforts is influenced by the recognition of two different audiences: the "old hands" and the "new hands."

Table 3.1: *Comparison of Venditti's Old and New Hands*

Old Hands	• already know and care about the cause, issue, or activity.
	• do not need convincing of the importance of the cause, issue, or activity.
	• are likely to respond positively when invited to participate when the "come on board" message is clear.
New Hands	• do not know about, care about, or previously supported the cause, issue, or activity.
	• need convincing of the importance or value of the cause, issue, or activity.
	• are unlikely to respond positively when invited to participate because the issue, cause, or activity is invisible to them until they see a connection to their own needs, interests, or desires.

As you can see in **Table 3.1**, the two populations are dramatically different. For that reason, any *one-size-fits-all* approach to motivational efforts is likely to be ineffective. Venditti (2001) describes two principles that address how to approach these populations.

The first approach is the *Accretion Principle*. It resembles a *magnet* attempting to pull others, both *old hands* and *new hands* to the values of "the cause." The expectation is that behavior of those pulled to the cause will align with expectations. This principle can work with *old hands* but is not effective with *new hands*.

The second principle, the *Agglutination Principle*, begins with a shift in focus. When invited to become a part of the cause, activity, or issue, *whose* values, interests, or goals are the driving force is critical. The question is asked, "What do others [the new hands] value?" The motivational message *is taken to the newcomers* with the intent to create a bond or attachment based on a genuine desire to integrate *new hands'* values and interests with *yours*.

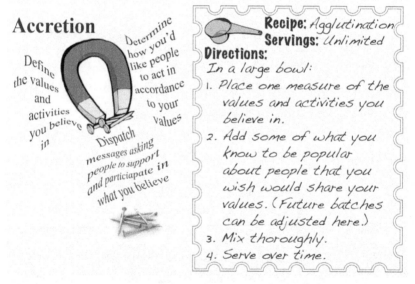

Figure 3.3. *Comparing the Principle of Accretion to the Principle of Agglutination.* Modification of Venditti (2001, 85).

There are two influencing factors for success of the Agglutination Principle—trust *and* the quality of the relationship between the populations. As teachers, we believe in, value, and devote ourselves to the educational process and system—*we are the old hands*. Our students, may or may not believe in, value, or have interest in investing their time, thoughts, and energy in the educational process or experiences that are required. They are the *new hands*—and, they are a captive audience.

You must seek to learn the values, beliefs, and interests of your students (your new hands). And you must choose to meet them rather than require they embrace your values, beliefs, and interests just because they're in your classroom.

Re-read the previous paragraph again. *It's in italics for a reason.* Go ahead, we'll wait…

Now that you've read that paragraph a second time, you can see that seeking the values, beliefs, and interests of newcomers *is* an opportunity to take a closer look at what drives humans to act or not act, invest or not invest, participate or not participate. If you consider your students as *new hands*, the interpretation of "unmotivated" can be addressed as a possible lack of awareness of what is valuable. Students often have a feeling of being outsiders whose values, interests, and goals are invisible. Without correction, this leads to a long-term absence of a relationship, or a poor relationship with the "old hand" in the room—that would be *you*!

A study of the relationship between school context, achievement, motivation, and academic engagement concluded that both emotional engagement and cognitive engagement were positively influenced by student perceptions of meaningfulness of subject matter. Activities provided by their teachers, as well as degree of relatedness of those activities to student goals, were additional influencing factors on this relationship (Wang, Eccles & Kenny 2013).

Students are rational beings—yes, even middle schoolers—although we have to admit it often appears as though the jury is still out on some. Their rationality leads them to figure out how to survive in an environment with minimal buy-in. We can list four outcomes of this type of thinking

- reliance on extrinsic rewards
- pursuit of short-term goals to the detriment of long-term goals
- compliance for the sake of expediency
- avoidance of negative consequences

The challenge for you is to find a starting point to engage the *new hands*. You'll need to adjust your instructional choices. And you'll need to adjust the design of the learning environment in appropriate and practical ways. Successful completion of these tasks increases the potential for students to connect to and value their learning opportunities. In essence, you are moving your students towards the intrinsic end of the motivational continuum.

The example of **Transforming a Common Activity** that follows showcases the learning factor of motivation.

Example of Transforming a Common Activity

The fully described and explained Transformed Activity is suitable for grades 4-10.

- **Common Science Assignment**: *Use your textbook or notes to answer the following questions about bony fish.*
    1. *Describe the movement of a bony fish while swimming.*
    2. *Explain how gills function in bony fish respiration.*
    3. *Why are bony fish scales covered with mucus?*
    4. *What is the function of the swim bladder (air bladder or gas bladder) in a bony fish?*
- **Common Social Science Assignment**: *Use your textbook or notes to answer the following questions about how a bill goes through Congress.*
    1. *How does a bill get to committee?*
    2. *What happens to a bill while it is in committee?*
    3. *Where does the bill go after it leaves committee?*
    4. *How does the bill finally become law?*
- **Common Math Assignment**: *Use your textbook or notes to answer the following questions about how to add unlike fractions.*
    1. *What is the first step in adding unlike fractions?*
    2. *How do you re-write the fractions based on your answer to question #1?*
    3. *What do you add to get your answer?*
    4. *What do you do before you have your final answer?*

Commentary: This assignment is completed as students look through their textbooks or notes. Information is copied from either source and written on the answer sheet with little regard to anything but "having the right answers." At best this is an example of **Engagement**. But, in truth, it's probably not much of that.

Example of the above as a Transformed Activity

My Life as a Fish

For this assignment, you will be asked to complete three parts in order as you produce a "story." Be sure to follow each step so you will have a chance at receiving full credit on this assignment.

Part 1: Write out one or a few word answers to each of the following questions.
1. *How does a fish swim?*
    a. *What fin is most important?*
    b. *In what direction does that fin move while the fish is swimming?*
2. *How does a fish breathe?*
    a. *What part of the fish's body is used in breathing?*
    b. *Where does the oxygen for the fish to breathe come from?*
3. *What are three reasons that a fish is covered with mucus?*
4. *Why do most bony fish have swim bladders?*
    a. *Where is the swim bladder located?*
    b. *How does the air in the bladder affect the fish?*

Commentary: Part 1 of the transformed activity looks suspiciously similar to the "common" version. And, as in that version, minimal **Engagement** is the only Learning Task. However, by providing more specific direction and encouraging short answers, student motivation is increased—*this is an assignment a student can complete successfully.*

Part 2: Now re-write your answers to the above questions as complete sentences.
Commentary: In Part 2, a second task that can be performed successfully by all is assigned to students. If nothing else, students might be curious about

why they have to do anything with the information, since "we already have the answer." The process is designed to motivate students to take on a **Creative Synthesis** task by providing a series of tasks at which they can be successful.

Part 3: *Write a short, fishy, fiction story in pencil. You should pretend that you are a talking fish that was floating motionless at a depth of two meters in a pond until you saw the worm (but not the hook!). You swam over to the worm and were just hooked by a person fishing in your pond. It's okay to use the sentences you wrote word-for-word, if they fit in your story like that.*

The requirements for the story include:

a. *Describe how you are swimming in the pond.*
b. *Tell about the food you tried to eat.*
c. *Explain how it felt when the hook hidden in the food poked into your mouth.*
d. *Include a dialog between you and the person who caught you as you are held in that person's hands.*
   • *Tell the person why you need to go back into the water quickly.*
   • *Tell the person why he should not touch your slimy scales any more than he has to before letting you go.*
e. *Explain how you can remain motionless at a depth you choose to the person who caught you.*

You must make a convincing argument for your release to the person that caught you. If you don't, part of the assessment of your paper will be you, as the fish, ending up filleted in a skillet! And, that is a fate you definitely want to avoid.

Commentary: By the time students are assigned Part 3, they have successfully completed enough of the writing assignment that the story-writing task is not a daunting one. Also, most students are motivated by the potential of using previous work (the sentences) without changing that work in what they see as another assignment.

This activity can be further extended to a "final draft," if desired. Also, allowing students to add pictures of their fish at various stages in the story, or even accepting "comic book" type stories with lots of art and fewer words, can add to the **Complexity** of the task.

Teacher Notes

- This assignment is specifically designed for portfolio use. After the assignment in pencil has been peer graded, it should be recorded and returned to students for final revision. The final draft would then be placed into the student's portfolio along with the parts of the assignment turned in previously.

- One check you will need to make is to be certain that each of the students has completed all three parts of the assignment. If you use a rubber stamp on the paper to show completion of a part, then looking for three stamps at the end of the assignment is all that is needed to give a grade for completeness.

- Students will need access to a biology, life science, or vertebrate zoology book to get the information necessary to answer the original questions. An alternate resource would be an encyclopedia. Of course, the Internet, correctly monitored, is a viable choice as well.

Answers to questions

1. Fish use their fins for swimming. a) The caudal (tail) fin; b) The caudal fin moves side-to-side.

2. The gills (or gill filaments) of a fish are used to take oxygen from the water in which the fish is swimming. b) gills; b) the water.

3. Mucous reduces friction for fish movement, it provides lubrication for the scales as they rub against each other during movement, and it is antiseptic.

4. Helps them float under water. a) inside the fish's body. b) the amount and concentration of the gasses in the bladder helps the fish control the depth at which it remains suspended in its environment.

- When checking the student papers for following the instructions, be sure that Part 2 includes complete sentences. Also, be sure to check for the five required points in Part 3.

- To increase **Engagement** and to add **Analysis** to the activity, have students follow the instructions below to evaluate stories written by other students. The purpose of the Group Scoring Pen (GSP) is to focus the group on listening when another group member is reading, since the GSP is the only writing utensil for the group.

-

1. Form groups as directed and put all pens and pencils away.
2. Get a Group Scoring Pen from your teacher.
3. Read your story out loud. The first reader is the person whose birthday is closet to today. Then read in clockwise order.
4. There are 5 (five) requirements to cover in the directions for the assignment. As your partners listen, they will stop you whenever they hear you discussing one of the required elements of the assignment.

For example:
1. When you describe how you are swimming in the pond, they will stop your reading.
2. When you are stopped, write the "letter" of the requirement directly on the paper on the words you were reading and circle it with the group scoring pen you received. In the case of how you are swimming, the correct mark on your paper would be a.
3. For requirement **d**, use the following symbols:
   Quick Return to Water = **d-Q**; Don't Touch the Mucus = **d-T**

The Elephant in the Room: *Influencing factors of disposition, attitude, and emotional intelligence*

At the beginning of this chapter, we asked you to answer Essential Question #4. Take a minute or two to review your previous response and revise it with any new thoughts or fresh insights you've gleaned so far. (Hopefully, you have at least *one!*)

Extrinsic motivation may more accurately be described as motivation triggered by singular or isolated events. *Intrinsic motivation* is a process. A process is not a single event, magic pill, one strategy or technique.

Question: What does it take to *make* someone want to learn, want to accomplish, want to invest time, thought, and energy over a period of time?

Question: What role does *motivation* play in building a learning environment that drives our students to personalize the goal of becoming a lifelong learner?

Hopefully, you have a glimmer of an idea of what you need to do to help your students towards the pearl of intrinsic motivation. Whether you think you have a glimmer or not, think back to **The Analogy**. One way that the Monarch helped her subjects to become self-motivators was by pulling back— she moved from the role of *information provider* to *facilitator* and eventually to *resource developer*. Record your discoveries of those roles, described in Chapter 2, in column three of your chart.

Earlier in the chapter, we assured you that we would not tackle the thirty-two theories that address human motivation as outlined by Martin E. Ford. While keeping that promise, we will provide a manageable and practical overview of possibly his most significant theoretical contribution to the field: Motivational Systems Theory (MST) (D. Ford, 1987; M. Ford and D. Ford, 1987). Ford (1992) explains that he was

motivated by the urgent need for a clear, coherent, and useful theory that could guide the efforts of scholars, professionals, and students concerned about, and interested in learning how to better address real-world problems with strong motivational underpinnings—problems such as academic underachievement and school dropout, low levels of work productivity and job satisfaction… (ix).

His Motivational Systems Theory is an integrative model. According to MST,

motivation is defined as the *organized patterning* [authors' emphasis] of three psychological functions that serve to direct, energize, and regulate goal-directed activity: personal goals, emotional arousal processes, and personal agency beliefs

(Ford, M. 1992, 3).

We've included a summary of sorts of the MST in two tables in the final section of this chapter titled, ***A Summary of Sorts***.

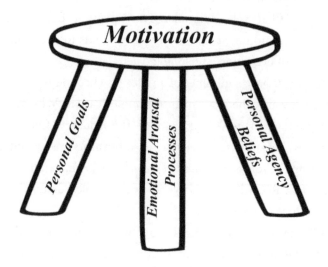

Figure 3.4. *Conceptual Picture of Motivation as the Patterning of Three Interacting Psychological Components.*

In the table below, two terms appear under Personal Agency Beliefs—*capability beliefs* and *context beliefs*. Capability beliefs will determine your answers to the following questions:

1. Am I capable of achieving this goal?
2. Do I have what it takes to accomplish this goal?

Capability beliefs are *expectancies.* In other words, they provide the answer to this question: *Do I have the personal capabilities needed to effectively accomplish this task?*

Context beliefs will determine your answers to the following questions:

1. Does my context provide me with the opportunity to try and achieve my goal?
2. Will my context make it easier or harder for me to attain my goal?

3. Can I trust this context to support me or cooperate with me in what I try to do, or will I be ignored/rejected/attacked?

Context beliefs are also *expectancies*. In other words, they provide the answer to this question: *Will the environment be responsive to **my** goal-attainment efforts?*

Table 3.2: *Summary of Motivation as Patterning*

Personal Goals	• Goals have a motivational impact if they become *personal* goals. • A goal cannot truly be imposed on anyone. It must be adopted as a personal goal for it to perform a direction function—it either leads to a desired result or avoids an undesirable result (as cited in M.Ford 1992, 74; D.H. Ford and Lerner 1992, 181-182).
Emotional Arousal Processes	Ford makes a clear distinction between emotional and non-emotional affective states. Emotions provide evaluative information on the following: 1. Problems 2. Opportunities of potential relevance that the problems represent 3. Preparations that help the individual deal with problems and opportunities
Personal Agency Beliefs	Personal agency beliefs are defined as anticipatory evaluations about whether one can achieve a goal—the student's expectation of success. This motivational component is expressed through two processes, *capability* and *context* beliefs. It is the interaction of both types of beliefs that determines whether a student activates or inhibits behaviors that assist in attaining a goal.

"He Said/She Said"

Dr. D: I think my head hurts.

Dr. J: Ha. Ha. Have you been doing all the STOP! activities?

Dr. D: Ha. Ha, right back at you. I've learned that following directions is a leading factor in the reduction of confusion. So, if motivation is all about *personal*—individuals deciding and emoting—what's my role as *teacher* in the process?

Dr. J: Well, your underlying role is a facilitator in the process. You want your students to develop motivational patterns and learn to make choices that are effective. Effective motivational patterns lead to success, and they endure beyond any academic class.

Dr. D: So, the teacher is a collaborator rather than a commander.

Dr. J: Nice analogy. Remember the old hands and new hands concept from Chapter 2?

Dr. D: Let's see if I've got this. The teacher's expertise is required for planning, providing, and coordinating experiences and opportunities, *and* anticipating contingencies that may influence the motivational *pattern* of a student.

Dr. J: Perhaps a bit verbose, but I think that's a good way to describe it.

Dr. D: Sounds like the teacher is a motivational interventionist.

Dr. J: Yes! That's a great way to look at it.

Dr. D: How hard can that be?

Dr. J: It's not necessarily difficult. As with any intervention, respect for the goals, emotions, and personal agency beliefs of the person to whom the intervention is directed impacts the effectiveness of that intervention.

Dr. D: That sounds a little like pie in the sky.

Dr. J: Don't give up on this, yet. Let's look at a model that illustrates how goals, emotions, and personal agency beliefs actually work together in real-life.

Richard Sagor's CBUPO Model

Richard Sagor's article, "Lessons from Skateboarders" (2002), introduces an acronym, CBUPO. Sagor studied motivation research, educational research, and conducted observations and discussions with teenagers. The focus of his study arose from the persistency of the skateboarders' behavior as they attempted to master the art of skateboarding.

He noted that in the specific example of skateboarders learning new tricks, the absence of extrinsic rewards did not dissuade them from persevering, struggling through challenges, and taking risks until they were successful.

Even though the typical skateboarder experienced a failure-to-success ratio of at least one hundred to one, the teenagers kept *working*. Poor attitudes were absent (the Emotional Arousal Process of MST). Repeated practice was a given. Personal goals (another MST component) were the catalyst for action. Effort and outcome were partnered with self-confidence that came from an assessment of personal power to effect change (the Personal Agency Beliefs of MST).

Why was this skateboarding scenario so different than what can be observed of students in educational settings of all kinds? Sagor provides a straightforward response to the questions uttered by many teachers.

1. What is it that motivates my students to spend hours attempting to master challenging sports or _____ or _____ (you can fill in the blanks)?
2. How can I get them to do the same with their studies?

His summative response is that all humans have five basic needs that if satisfied will fuel and propel one to continue striving for mastery in whatever endeavor chosen. See **Figure 3.5**.

When you deliberately plan to meet all five of those basic needs in your classroom, the outcome is almost always self-motivated students.

A Summary of Sorts

We've circled back to **Essential Question #4** (Again! Hmmm. Think about *that*.): *What is the target? When students leave my classroom they will be* _____.

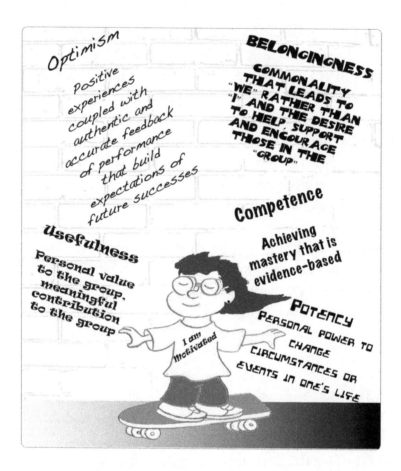

Figure 3.5: *Sagor's Five Basic Needs.*

Did your original or revised response include the descriptor *motivated*? Hopefully, that simple word evokes more shades of understanding of a complex process than before you read this chapter. We also hope that you have even more building materials to use as you create the most effective teaching and learning environment.

Table 3.3a and **Table 3.3b** are the summary tables promised for the Martin Ford's MST.

Motivation is a complex *process* that requires more than awareness and reflection. It requires analysis and intentional action with specific goals or targets in focus. There is so much more that can be said on this topic.

Table 3.3a: *Motivational Systems Theory: Core Ideas (1)*

The Principle of Unitary Functioning	• One always deals with a whole person in context
The Motivational Triumvirate Principle	• Goals, emotions, and personal agency beliefs must all be influenced to facilitate motivation
Goals	• Little else matters if there is no relevant goal in place • Goals must be clear and compelling to transform concerns into intentions • Multiple goals can strengthen motivation substantially • Multiple goals must be aligned rather than in conflict to enhance motivation • Goals lose their potency in the absence of clear and informative feedback
Standards	• Flexible standards protect against demotivation and facilitate self-improvement • Challenging but attainable standards enhance motivation

Adapted from *Motivating Humans: Goals, Emotions, and Personal Agency Beliefs*; Martin E. Ford (1992).

Again, this chapter provides an introduction, and we suggest further study to inform your professional practice. In addition to summarizing the MST, the tables that bracket this paragraph provide you with a place to begin further study.

Not hammer-strokes, but dance of the water sings pebbles into perfection.

Rabindranath Tagore, 1861-1941

Table 3.3b: *Motivational Systems Theory: Core Ideas (2)*

Emotions	• Strong emotions indicate and facilitate strong motivational patterns
Relationships	• Relationships are as important as techniques
Personal Agency Beliefs (PABs)	• Clear, specific evidence is needed to influence capability and context beliefs • PABs ultimately require real skills and a truly responsive environment • If a person is capable, just try to get them started
Change	• Incremental change is easier and safer • Transform only with care and as a last resort [Transform in this context refers to experiences that are dramatic and designed to shock, to escalate situations to a level that initiates sudden but dramatic change and must be reserved for extreme cases.] • There are many ways to motivate humans—if progress is slow, keep trying! • People must be treated with respect to produce enduring motivational effects

Adapted from *Motivating Humans: Goals, Emotions, and Personal Agency Beliefs*; Martin E. Ford (1992).

Once again, it's time to revisit **The Analogy** chart you are working on. In the third column, record any instances where you find support for the motivational theory, practices, and processes from this chapter.

A Closing Quote

... How could someone ignore [your teaching methods]? They can't! To not take advantage of it would be dumb. It would take a "lazy dunce" to just sit there... I refuse to be a lazy dunce. Not just in [your class], but in any class... [Once] you asked something to the effect of," Why were your grades so blah last semester and so much better this semester?" That really felt good. Someone did care, after all. It may have been only one person, but that's all it took. I was beginning to give up on my good efforts, but I can't let you down. More importantly, I can't let myself down, thanks to you.

HG: High School Student

References for Chapter 3

Csikszentmihalyi, Mihaly. 1990. Flow: The Psychology of Optimal Experience. New York: Harper & Row.

_____. 2008. Flow: The Psychology of Optimal Experience. New York: Harper Perennial Modern Classics.

Csikszentmihalyi, M. and Barbara Schneider. 2000. Becoming Adult: How Teenagers Prepare *for the World of Work*. New York, New York: Basic Books.

Ford, Donald H. 1987. *Humans as Self-Constructing Living Systems: A Developmental Perspective on Behavior and Personality.* Hillsdale, New Jersey: Lawrence Erlbaum.

Ford, Donald H., and Richard M. Lerner. 1992. *Developmental Systems Theory: An Integrative Approach.* Newbury Park, California: Sage.

Ford, Martin E., and Donald H. Ford, eds. 1987. *Humans as Self-Constructing Living Systems: Putting the Framework to Work.* Hillsdale, New Jersey: Lawrence Erlbaum.

Ford, Martin E. 1992. *Motivating Humans: Goals, Emotions, and Personal Agency Beliefs.* Newbury Park, California: Sage Publications.

Hektner, Joel M., and Mihaly Csikszentmihalyi. 1996. "A Longitudinal Exploration of Flow and Intrinsic Motivation in Adolescents." Paper presented at the Annual Meeting of the American Educational Research Association. New York, New York. April 8-12.

Sagor, Richard. 2002. "Lessons from Skateboarders." *Educational Leadership* 60(1): 34-38.

Scherer, Marge. 2002. "Do Students Care About Learning? A Conversation with Mihaly Csikszentmihalyi." *Educational Leadership* 60 (1): 12-17.

Venditti, Phillip. 2001. "A New Motivational Principle for Educators." *Educational Horizons* (Winter): 85-88.

Wang, Ming Te, and Jacquelynne S. Eccles. 2013. "School Context, Achievement Motivation, and Academic Engagement: A Longitudinal Study of School Engagement Using a Multidimensional Perspective." *Learning and Instruction* 28: 12-23.

Chapter 4

USE YOUR BRAIN, NOT MINE... PLEASE.

HELPING STUDENTS TO WANT TO THINK. IT'S NOT SIMPLE... YOU HAVE TO BE STRATEGIC

Chapter Overview - Critical Thinking Island

The third bridge ends at **Critical Thinking Island**. On this island, you'll be looking at why the balance of challenge and support is critical in a classroom environment. With that as a foundation, you'll investigate the importance of student perception of both work and play and how that can be used to your advantage. The importance of helping your students to learn to function and appreciate when they are stretched to an appropriate distance from their comfort zones is the final in our trifecta of key features of this island. We'll end our tour by presenting a tool, the Cognitive Rigor Matrix, which you can use to help you chart your path.

A Quote to Kickstart Your Thinking

> Students in this course were expected to think things through and make independent decisions. This was a revolutionary method [to me], and, at first, I would experience a short period of frustration. After all, students in high school are accustomed to having someone walk them step-by-step through whatever problem they are asked to solve. However, knowing that I ultimately had to figure out the assignment on my own allowed for a great sense of motivation, and I was internally driven to solve whatever activity was in front of me. Whenever I would actually "solve" and finish an activity I obtained a different sense of pride than in any of my other classes—I knew that I had done it on my own. I was capable of understanding with minimal assistance and this self-reliance became the basis for my interest in the topics. This method is one that I use every day in my university courses.
>
> **BT: PhD Candidate, University of Laverne**

Revisiting Key Points from Previous Chapters

While we're pretty sure you've been on top of all we've asked you to do and are confident of your retention of the content, to help frame this chapter, we begin by revisiting three key points from previous chapters.

The basic principles of the Gradual Release of Responsibility Model were discussed in detail in Chapter 2. They surface again as you consider how to attain the proper balance between supporting, guiding, and challenging your students and requiring their active participation in, and ownership of, their own learning. This leads us to consider the next of our Essential Questions.

Essential Question #5: *What type of thinking environment is necessary to reach the target? A thinking environment that is_____.*

Another way to phrase the question is, "What are some characteristics of a teaching/thinking environment that inspire learning and provide the best conditions for achievement?"

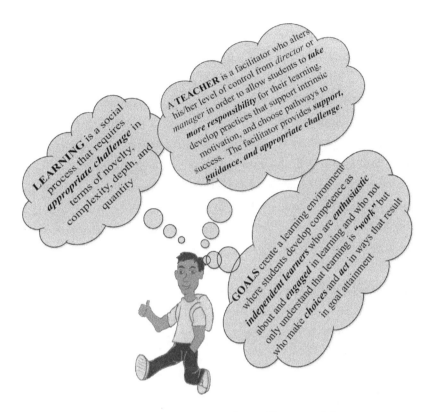

Figure 4.1. *Key Points from Chapters 1-3.*

 Take a few moments and respond to both versions of the above question.

The Balance of Challenge and Support

Challenge and support are companion elements that require careful and frequent assessment as to both quality and quantity. **Challenge** refers to a learning experience that requires a high level of independence and expectations—novelty is a valued component. Challenge is dependent on the knowledge and skill base of the learner as well as the features of the environment. In other words, an *appropriate challenge must be context-embedded.*

Support has many faces that are more process-oriented than content-oriented. Resources, materials, collaborative activities, and differentiated instruction all qualify as *support* when appropriately matched to the student and the learning task. A mismatch in any of these areas diminishes what *you intended as support.* Your mismatched effort becomes an obstruction or hindrance.

If there is a difference in your perception of the necessity of the support you provide and the student's perception of what is needed as support, the result is, at best, annoyance—as students now see the learning experience as too easy or unnecessary. If students perceive a need for specific support, *and you fail to perceive that need and provide that specific support,* the result is far worse than annoyance. When this level of disconnect between your perceptions and your students' perceptions continues over time and/or in a variety of contexts, students enter into cycles of self-defeating attitudes and self-defeating actions.

Fill in the blanks with short statements. 1) If one is appropriately challenged, he/she feels or is willing to _____. 2) If one has appropriate support, he/she feels or is willing to _____.

Learning as <u>Work</u>

In Chapter 3, we found that students who evaluated their activities as both work and play were more likely to go to college or successfully transition to the work world. Additionally, they enjoyed the activities *even with* the responsibilities and challenges associated with them—work and play were essential companions in this process.

Let's take some time to investigate *work.* Consider this partial list of definitions of work:

- activity in which one *exerts* strength or faculties to do or perform something
- *sustained* physical or mental *effort* to overcome obstacles and *achieve* an objective or result
- something produced or accomplished by effort, exertion, or *exercise* of skill
- something produced by the exercise of creative talent or *expenditure* of creative effort: artistic production (ex. an early *work* by a major writer)

Exerts, sustained, effort, achieve, exercise, expenditure are terms that drive the definitions. They indicate that *action* is required for the achievement of an endeavor. Work done by your students occurs at the intersections of their competencies, skills, abilities, and proficiencies. When you are contemplating on how you can encourage your students to work, consider the following questions:

- What balance must exist between challenge, support, work, **and** *play*?
- What are the incentives your students have to do any *work*?
- What's your role in designing a learning environment that capitalizes on your students' knowledge, skills, and abilities?
- What can you do to transition your students from "using your brain" (as the sage on the stage) to wanting to think for themselves—to do the *work* of learning?
- What can you do so your students embrace the idea that work as a process is valuable in any context and is linked to success in achieving personal goals?

 Jot down a quick answer to this: If you asked your students what they were *working* for, what would they say?

If you don't like the answer you just wrote, keep reading—we've got some information and ideas that *will help you* re-write what you wrote. If you liked your answer, keep reading—we've got some information and ideas that *might help you* re-write what you wrote. Bottom line: regardless of what you wrote, **keep reading**—we've got some information and ideas that *will help you* regardless of your response.

Just Manageable Difficulties

I believe we are not content with what we already know and can do; we want action and growth—opportunities to explore our competence and mastery.

(**Brim** 1992, 10)

Humans are designed to seek growth, mastery, and experiences at what Nicholas Hobbs (1974) refers to as "just manageable difficulties." Working on tasks at a level that capitalizes on our abilities, goals, and interests while *stretching* us just the right amount is what keeps us going and in the frame of mind of *play* and positive *affect*. The *right amount* of stretching takes into account the relationship between *risk and reward* and the *value* we place on succeeding at the task.

The concept of just manageable difficulties echoes Vygotsky's Zone of Proximal Development (**ZPD**). By definition, the ZPD refers to

> …the distance between the actual developmental level as determined by independent problem solving [without guided instruction] and the level of potential development as determined through problem solving under an adult's guidance or in collaboration with more capable peers [i.e., acting as more knowledgeable others]…
>
> (Vygotsky 1978).

Vygotsky describes "good learning" as that which is *in advance of development*. In the classroom, this means that instruction should be designed to appropriately exceed the level of student development—where students consider themselves to be for a specific task. For example, the student statement from our interpretation of GRRM, "Partner With Me, I'll Take the Lead," can be ineffective in promoting growth to a higher developmental level. This is where you want an imbalance between where your students think they are and where you want them to be. Without a proper imbalance—where the student feels stretched—development stagnates.

Initial mastery *is the stepping-stone* for subsequent development of more in-depth learning and understanding. However, *stretching* your students by providing tasks that are just beyond what they have mastered is required for further development. Instruction that *overshoots* the ZPD is ineffective in promoting developmental growth. Such instruction and activities are *incomprehensible* to your students and are *unreachable* or *unattainable* at their present level of competence.

The most effective teaching and learning states occur within the ZPD that represents, for example, skills that are **slightly beyond** your students' demonstrated level of development. Without stretching your students beyond what they know they can do, development does not continue—your students cannot further develop on their own. However, with the guidance, support, encouragement, cooperation, and collaboration with *more knowledgeable others*—you or more advanced students—your students can develop to the next level.

"What I can do *with your help* today, I will be able to do *by myself* tomorrow" is the type of thinking that sets up the next opportunity for a *just manageable difficulty*. Notice that this process will continue to be effective if the more knowledgeable other, *you* as the teacher in this case, continues to accurately analyze your students' actual level of competence and quality of thinking.

Stephen Krashen, a pioneer in second language acquisition theory, developed the *Monitor Theory*. Monitor Theory includes five hypotheses (Krashen, 1982; 2004). While all five are important tenets in language acquisition, only the *Comprehension Hypothesis* (originally called the *Input Hypothesis*) is pertinent to our discussion. The *Comprehension Hypothesis* proposes that a second language is acquired when messages are one step beyond current proficiency levels: i + 1. In this equation, the **i** represents the current stage of linguistic competence—the **+1** represents the *just right amount of stretching* that will allow for improvement and progression along the continuum to fluency. Input that is beyond the **+1** in difficulty may be incomprehensible to the learner. Incomprehensible input is ineffective for advancing linguistic competence.

As in language acquisition, the key to advancing your students along the continuum of competence in your subject matter is for you to accurately determine current levels of competence. After that assessment, your task is to provide a learning environment that is *one step beyond those levels*. We've cut the amount of reading on this topic for you by providing **Figure 4.2**.

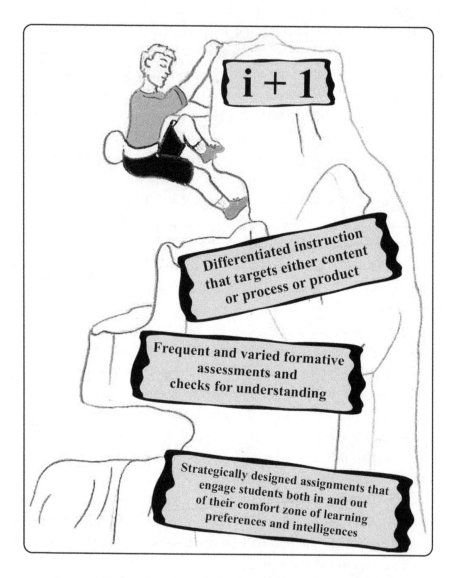

Figure 4.2: *Operating in the Zone of Proximal Development.*

"He Said/She Said"

Dr. D: All this is on how to get students to want to think. Right?

Dr. J: It's the start of that, yes.

Dr. D: I'm not sure I've been keeping up.

Dr. J: What do you remember so far?

Dr. D: Ummm. Students require a learning environment that is challenging.

Dr. J: And...

Dr. D: There has to be support available for the student.

Dr. J: Yes, and how challenging should the tasks be?

Dr. D: Kind of hard, but not too hard.

Dr. J: I'm afraid you're missing the specifics. Remember the environment must be challenging but not defeating or beyond the reach of the students.

Dr. D: I was heading there.

Dr. J: Great... and students also have to know they will have a safety net when practicing. In other words—

Dr. D: The teacher has to step back, though—at appropriate times.

Dr. J: The key is *knowing* when it is "appropriate." The process requires informed educators—truly reflective practitioners. And, of course, on-going assessment is essential.

Dr. D: Of course. Assessment should always drive instruction. It's also my experience that students like variety in assignments.

Dr. J: Very true. Especially when the environment is supportive. Even though they realize that learning requires mental work, students are willing to risk, to try, because they know they won't be left in the dust.

Dr. D: Hmmm. So, when J.S., one of my former students wrote me and said, *In your class I was willing to try all the assignments, no matter how hard I thought they were at first, because I knew that you would never give us any assignment we couldn't do,"* it meant I was on the right track?

Dr. J: Definitely on the right track, and aren't I smart for writing this book with you! If you take a look at Figure 4.3, you'll see a summary of the chapter so far.

Dr. D: As you wish.

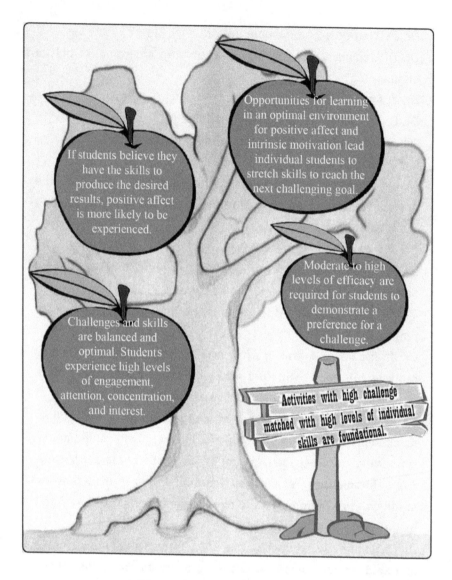

Figure 4.3. *Fruit for Thought.*

We set our levels of effort to accord with our beliefs about our capacities—how intelligent, strong, healthy, vigorous, wealthy, creative... we think we are.

(**Brim** 1992, 35)

Building students' capacity, their ability and desire to do the work it takes to learn, rests in large part on residing in a thriving environment. In an appropriate environment, opportunities are available to practice and develop different intellectual skills and interact with tasks that require thinking of varying depth and complexity.

Next, we'll explore a concept that will support you as you continue to transform your classroom into an environment where students want to think for themselves. In such an environment, your students are committed to increasing their competence in your subject area. Ultimately, you want your students to accurately self-identify as purposeful and effective creative thinkers.

Rigor

 Write your definition of *rigor*. Then list 3-5 observable and measureable examples in your practice/teaching to support your definition.

Rigor is a noun that is used often in educational settings where it carries a positive connotation—an admirable level of difficulty in content and process. Ironically, definitions of rigor are less than positive:

- harsh inflexibility in opinion, temper, or judgment
- the quality of being unyielding or inflexible
- severity of life
- strict precision

Rigor mortis is a companion dictionary entry. That definition reads: rigidity or torpor of organs or tissue that prevents response to stimuli. By the way, if you look up the definition for *rigorous*, it isn't any more appealing.

The contrast between the educational connotation and the dictionary definitions often mirrors a contrast of thinking between you and your students.

Be honest...which version of the definition for rigor is the operational definition of your students?

You've probably sat in professional development meetings where the lack of rigor was given for, oh, let's say, low test scores; or, perhaps, grade inflation;

or, the failure of your graduates in college. A common mantra is: *Make your courses rigorous!*

In *Teaching What Matters Most: Standards and Strategies for Raising Student Achievement*, the following definition of rigor is provided:

> Rigor is the goal of helping students develop the capacity to understand content that is complex, ambiguous, provocative, and personally or emotionally challenging
>
> (Strong, Silver, Matthew, and Perini 2001).

That's more like it. Seeing *rigor* as thoroughness, challenging, stretching, intense, and invigorating is something you can believe in.

This is the real secret of life—to be completely engaged with what you are doing in the here and now. And instead of calling it work, realize it is play.

Alan Wilson Watts

Categorizing and Leveling Thinking

Commonly referred to as *Bloom's Taxonomy of Educational Objectives*, this widely used classification system was actually developed by a team (Bloom et al. 1956). Under the leadership of Benjamin S. Bloom, a group of measurement specialists was commissioned to design a means to facilitate the sharing of test items between universities. Creating a bank of test items would allow universities to measure the same educational objectives and goals and compare the interuniversity results directly. Towards that end, efforts were focused on the creation of a classification system of the cognitive, affective, and psychomotor domains.

The original work on the cognitive domain was published in 1956 and has been used extensively in curriculum writing, lesson planning, and assessment development. There are six major categories (often identified as levels) for the cognitive domain. They are ordered from simple to complex and concrete to abstract. The categories are hierarchical and considered cumulative. The assumption was that mastery of each of the *simpler* categories was **prerequisite** for mastery of the next or higher level category.

The Taxonomy supports the notion that students can *know* about a topic in different ways and at different levels of complexity. The levels (nouns) are assigned to learning tasks based on the main action verb of a learning task or question. For example, "*compare* the causes of WWI and WWII" or "*compare* a square and a rectangle." Notice both tasks require "*compare*"—the verb *compare* itself does not indicate the complexity of the task. While Bloom's Taxonomy has served educators well throughout the years, a revision in 2001 provided additional refinement for improved analysis of educational objectives (Anderson and Krathwohl 2001).

Table 4.1a: *The Old and New Bloom's Taxonomy*

Changes to Bloom's Taxonomy	
1956	**2001**
Evaluation	*Create*
Synthesis	**Evaluate**
Analysis	Analyze
Application	Apply
Comprehension	Understand
Knowledge	Remember
Noun → to Verb Form	
In the 2001 version, **Evaluation/***Evaluate* and **Synthesis/***Create* have switched relative positions in the hierarchy.	

The revision retained the six original categories; however, three of the categories were renamed. The order of two of the categories was interchanged and the category names were changed to the verb form (example: *knowledge* was renamed *remember*). The subcategories or descriptors were also renamed as cognitive processes to characterize the depth and breadth of each category. The revision reinforces the interaction of content taught. This is distinguished by the different types of knowledge required—factual, procedural, metacognitive, conceptual—and the thought processes needed for demonstration of learning.

Table 4.1b: *The Original and The Revised Bloom*

Original Bloom's Taxonomy (1956)	Revised Bloom Process Dimensions (2001)
Category/Level: *Synthesis* (noun) **Descriptor:** Put parts together to form a new whole	**Category/Level:** *Evaluating* (verb) **Descriptor:** Make judgments based on criteria and standards
Category/Level: *Evaluation* (noun) **Descriptor:** Judge value of material for a given purpose	**Category/Level:** *Creating* (verb) **Descriptor:** Put elements together to form a coherent or functioning whole; reorganizing elements into a new pattern or structure through generating, planning, or producing

As of 2014, the taxonomy retains its hierarchical nature in terms of complexity of cognitive processes. However, it recognizes that the fluid nature of thinking may require a mixing or crossing of the categories. This final inclusion of the fluidity of thinking is the focus of what follows.

The Depth of Knowledge Model (DOK model) was developed to systematically analyze the alignment between standards and standardized assessments. It has since become a valuable tool for teachers and curriculum specialists to use in the analysis and revision of poorly aligned or ineffective curricular elements and assessments. The model is based on the assumption that curricular elements (e.g., activities, assignments, assessments) can be grouped based on interpreting the cognitive demands required of students to produce an acceptable response, complete a task, or answer a question. The grouping uses *depth of knowledge* to describe the level of cognitive demand. The DOK consists of four ways to describe or name how a student might interact with content [see **Tables 4.2a – 4.2d**] (Webb 2002).

The DOK model does *not* put the emphasis on Bloom's taxonomic levels, in other words *the type of thinking* a student engages in while completing a task (e.g., assignment, activity, assessment). Instead, the focus is on *how deep the understanding* of content must be in order for students to *successfully interact* with the task. Both the *complexity of the content of the task* (e.g., interpreting narrative text vs. expository text) and *the depth of understanding of the content* we expect students to demonstrate are used to determine what DOK level is assigned to a task. An example of this concept is the level of understanding required in the solving of routine vs. non-routine problems.

The model considers the complexity, or degree of abstractness, of the cognitive processes required to successfully complete a task, create a product, or answer a question. This is not the only consideration, however. The key is *consistency in alignment* between the degree of:

1. **complexity of the standard**—the knowledge and skill objectives/targets
2. **difficulty of the task**—the curricular element designed for students to develop or demonstrate their knowledge and skills
3. **cognitive rigor and reliability of the assessment**—assessing what it is supposed to *and* at the level of thinking required by the standard *and* practiced via the task

All three must be aligned if your students are to reach the levels of mastery with content and skills expected by increasingly rigorous standards (Webb 1997; 2002).

The work of Bloom resulted in a *taxonomy*—a progression of levels of understanding. In contrast, Webb's work describes the rigor and relevance resulting from *analysis* and ***alignment*** of standards, learning tasks, and assessments. The critical question to answer when you use the DOK model is, "Where is the complexity in this task?" (Webb 2005; 2006). Remember, to answer that question, you must consider both the *quality* of mental processing required and the *complexity* of the content. When used correctly, the Depth of Knowledge model encourages rigor. Where Bloom *sorts* thinking levels, DOK *interweaves* them.

We've provided some background for the DOK model. The iconic circular representation of the DOK levels/descriptors is accessible via the **Resources** page of our website. **Table 4.2a-d** provides an overview of the four levels and examples of tasks at each level.

Table 4.2a. *DOK Level 1*

DOK Level 1: Recall & Reproduction	
Description of DOK Level	**Potential activities**
• Requires students to recall or reproduce information • *Little transformation or extended processing of knowledge required by task* • Student either knows the answer or does not. Not "figured out" or "solved"	• *Working with facts, definitions, terms, performance of a simple process, procedure, or formula* • Make a timeline • *Identify elements of music using music terminology* • Make a chart showing… • *Write a brief outline and explain story elements* • Identify basic rules for playing a game • *Paraphrase a chapter in a book* • Use a dictionary to find the meaning of…

Table 4.2b. *DOK Level 2*

DOK Level 2: Basic Skills & Concepts	
Description of DOK Level	**Potential activities**
• Requires students to go beyond a description or explanation of recalled information to describe or explain a "why," "how," or result. Use of information from a different context from one in which it was learned • *Requires students to make decisions on how to approach problem or question* • More than one cognitive process/step	• *Compare desert and tropical environments* • Identify and summarize major events, problems, solutions, conflicts in literary text • *Explain the cause-effect of historical events* • Construct a model to demonstrate how something works or looks • *Write an explanation about the topic for others* • Measurement task that occurs over a period of time and requires collecting/organizing data to display on a simple table or graph • *Use context cues to identify the meaning of unfamiliar words* • *Predict a logical outcome based on a reading*

Table 4.2c. *DOK Level 3*

DOK Level 3: Strategic Thinking & Reasoning	
Description of DOK Level	**Potential activities**
• Requires students to coordinate knowledge & skill from multiple subject-matter areas to carry out processes and reach a solution • *Students solve abstract, complex, or non-routine problems* • Often allows for more than one possible answer • *Stating one's reasoning characterizes tasks that fall into this category* • Explain, generalize, or connect ideas	• Determine author's purpose and describe how it affects the interpretation of a reading selection • *Summarize information from multiple sources to address a topic* • Use a Venn diagram that shows how topics are the same or different • *Prepare a report on a topic of study.* • Prepare and conduct a debate. • Make a booklet about rules you see as important. Convince others • *Solve a multiple-step problem and provide support with a mathematical explanation that justifies the answer*

Table 4.2d. *DOK Level 4*

DOK Level 4: Extended Thinking	
Description of DOK Level	**Potential Activities**
• Requires students to make connections, relate ideas within the content or among content areas, and select or devise one approach among many alternatives on how the situation can be solved • *Often requires an extended time period to accomplish* • Students engage in conducting investigations of complex real-world problems or unpredictable outcomes • *High cognitive demand and very complex*	• *Gather, analyze, organize, and interpret information from multiple sources to draft a reasoned report* • Analyze author's craft (style, bias, literary techniques, point of view) • *Write a jingle to advertise a new product* • Apply information to solve ill-defined or novel situations • *Conduct research and formulate and test a hypothesis over time*

Sources for Table 4a-d: (Webb 1997; 1999; 2002; 2005; 2009 & Hess 2012).

Let's pause here and make sure we're all on the same page regarding the DOK Model. **Table 4.3** is another visual describing some DOK concepts from a different perspective.

Table 4.3. *Selected DOK Concepts*

Selected Concepts from the Depth of Knowledge Model

Concept One: It is the **complexity** *of a task* **not** *the difficulty of that task that is used to determine the level of DOK assigned.*

A "DOK definition" of difficulty might read: *How many students can answer a question.* Let's look at a pair of examples to help cement this idea.

Example	Analysis
"How many of you know the definition of analyze?"	If most/all students know the answer, it is **not difficult**. This is DOK level 1: Recall.
"How many of you know the definition of exegesis?"	If few students know the answer, it **is** **difficult** but *still* DOK level 1: Recall

Concept Two: DOK is **NOT** *determined by the verb, but the context in which the verb is used and the depth of thinking required of the student.*

Example	Analysis
Compare is included in both DOK level 2 and DOK level 3.	You must analyze what comes after the verb to determine the mental processing required of the student to successfully complete the task and so the DOK category.

Concept Three: No activity or assignment is automatically or permanently designated to any one of the 4 DOK levels.

Analysis

You, the teacher, *determine* the complexity of the task and set(s) the level of prior knowledge required, and the mental processes required.

Concept Four: While it might seem advantageous to design all instruction to meet Depth of Knowledge Level 4 (Extended Thinking), the **goal** *is to provide students with a variety of learning opportunities across the four levels.*

Analysis

Be selective. Remember the importance of balance between challenge and support when crafting learner outcomes.

Now, it is your turn. Review the DOK information and assign a level to each of the following examples. We have provided the answers at the end of the chapter, but please take a shot at this on your own before you check our answers—even if you feel it's maxing out your personal ZPD:

1. Describe four characteristics of mammals.
2. Describe how the events that led to World War I and World War II are alike and how they are different.
3. Describe the most significant legislation for students with special needs.

What? Two STOPs in a row! Arraugh!!

Relax already. *There's a method to this madness.*

 Look back over your personal definition and examples of *rigor*. Revise that definition based on information from this section, "Categorizing and Leveling Thinking"

You may feel that the preceding **STOP!** stretched you beyond your comfort zone because the level of challenge and support were out of balance for you. You may be struggling with the question, "How can I effectively use this information from both Bloom's Taxonomy and the DOK model?"

We're going to add another level of support by describing a model that connects Bloom's work to Webb's—the Cognitive Rigor Matrix (Hess 2006a; 2006b).

Cognitive Rigor Matrix (CRM)

We have discussed the importance of balance *between challenge and support,* that *learning is work,* and the concept of *just manageable difficulties.* We did this to provide you with materials to construct an effective and engaging teaching and learning environment.

- What does *balance* look like when addressing the type of thinking that is required of students?
- Is *balance* the goal—equal amounts of assignments that require students to *think within* the different categories and levels?

Karin K. Hess (2006a; 2006b) developed the Cognitive Rigor Matrix (CRM), which superimposes Bloom's Taxonomy and Webb's Depth of Knowledge Levels. The superimposition is not as simple as a perfect one-to-one correspondence, but it does provide a clear and useful strategy to analyze curriculum, plan instruction, and implement assessments. The CRM is a tool for examining the depth of understanding required for different tasks that may first appear to be at the same level of complexity. It's also used to categorize assignments/learning activities that appear prominently in curriculum and instruction (Hess et al. 2009, 3).

Table 4.4. *Cognitive Rigor Matrix Template*

DOK Level/ Bloom (Rev)	1 Recall & Re-production	2 Basic Skills & Concepts	3 Strategic Thinking & Reasoning	4 Extended Thinking
Remember				
Understand				
Apply				
Analyze				
Evaluate				
Create				****

Of particular value to you as a classroom teacher is the application of the matrix to a series of assignments implemented across time. For example, computing the answer for a single step mathematical problem would be categorized as Bloom's category of *Apply* and *DOK Level 1* [**DOK-1, Bloom 3/ Apply**] or the (**1, 3**) cell of the CRM.

Once analyzed and categorized, consideration can be given to if and how to modify the assignment to require a different level of cognitive rigor. Plotting several assignments, by placing them in the appropriate cell of the CRM, reveals patterns of instructional emphasis and focus of learning in the classroom. It *is* the thinking environment you have created for your students.

What you see when you look at your completed plot is what your students perceive as the level of thinking required in your class. *This is the thinking environment you have created for your students.* You should consider this as prized information as a teacher committed to purposeful instructional choices because it allows you to modify assignments, or portions thereof, and engage students in a variety of thinking strategies—all based on *evidence*. This is an assessment of your instructional choices, and *it is what is driving your instruction*.

An 8.5" x 11" copy of **Table 4.4** and a completed CRM for some portion of each core content area are available to you via our website. We encourage you to access them and begin with one unit of your instruction. Place each of your assignments, activities, and assessments from that unit in the appropriate cell of the blank matrix. The pattern that emerges is a snapshot of the rigor and balance of your current curriculum.

We hope that we have convinced you of the value of analyzing the thought processes you require of your students. Stop reading, access the matrices, and begin the process. Remember, your goal is to provide balance across the categories of thinking in the matrix. *The goal is not to fill up the lower right-hand corner only*—there must be a balance between types of assignments and level of cognitive rigor required by your assignments and assessments.

You now have tools to reframe and analyze your instructional planning from the perspective of depth and complexity of thinking required. Keep in mind that you are working at maintaining the balance of learning as work and play. The proverb, "All work and no play..." and Aesop's fable of the "Grasshopper and the Ant" are examples of what happens if either work or play is out of balance. Your students deserve the best you can provide for them—sometimes that's work; other times it's play. Remember, your students need a balance of what *they see* as both *work and play*—ideally in the same task!

This chapter emphasized the highlighted portion of the first part of our definition of *learning*: *a social process that requires* **appropriate challenge in terms of novelty, complexity, depth, and quantity**. Revisit **Figure 4.1**.

The chapter title, "Use YOUR Brain, Not Mine… Please," implies that you know not only *what* your students should be *using* their brain for but also *how* and *why* they are doing what they are doing. That requires accurate, on-going, and systematic analysis of the standards that drive curriculum development, instructional planning, and assessment instruments. Competence in identifying and categorizing *levels* of thinking and knowledge of cognitive processes is foundational to effective instruction and academic success for your students.

> As educators become more skilled at recognizing the elements and dimensions of cognitive rigor and analyzing its implications for instruction and assessment, they can provide learning opportunities that benefit all students, across all subject areas and grade levels. In essence, the role of a school system is to prepare students by providing them with an aligned curriculum with differentiated emphasis on each of the four depth of knowledge levels
>
> (Hess et al. 2009).

Before reading the Example of Transforming a Common Activity, it's time to travel back to the Kingdom in **The Analogy**. This time you'll consider the Monarch and her Subjects' perception of *work* and *play*. Use the third column to record *evidence* and *rationale* that the Monarch's choices support the following statement,

Learning is optimized when students are involved in activities that require complex thinking and the application of knowledge

(Hess et al. 2009).

And now, on to the *transformed* activity…

Example of Transforming a Common Activity

This example of transforming an activity is "outside the box" and isn't linked to *any* specific discipline or grade level. Instead of a single assignment as the example, this section describes a transformation process that is useful in areas of assessment. Since this chapter is all about ZPD, and other models of how you can help students want to **work** to learn, it seemed like a good place to insert a description of the process we call *Developing Transitional Questions*.

There is a high probability that the bulk of assessments your students have experienced has been at lower taxonomic levels. To expect students to blossom suddenly into great critical thinkers able to provide cogent, coherent answers to conceptual prompts posed in your class is unrealistic. There is a need to *transition* from factual to conceptual assessment prompts. This "lack of transitioning" is another area where teachers often unknowingly *facilitate* the lack of quality in student answers. We recommend that you begin preparing your students for conceptual prompts by providing *transitional* prompts early in your course.

Let's start by defining transitional prompts as *those whose stem is stated in conceptual verbiage* (provides a challenge) *but which also include "clues" or "hints" for students* (provides support) *as to the direction a response to the prompt might take.* Sutman suggests:

> In order to provide students with the opportunity to think about and apply [your content area] concepts and to formulate complete thoughts [when writing answers], teachers should pose open-ended questions for them to answer. *Assistance can take the form of providing references* [authors' emphasis], helping students to use [appropriate content area vocabulary] to express their questions and answers; and helping them develop investigations that will lead to answers… [T]his approach may result in coverage of less content, [however] students will have a deeper understanding of the material that is covered, and will, ultimately, learn more because they learned not only some… concepts but also how to problem solve
>
> (Sutman et al. 1993, 3).

Although Sutman is writing specifically about limited language abilities, we can consider most of our students to be "inexperienced critical thinkers." We can provide "reference points" of differing degree. For example a transitional prompt might include any one of three options shown in **Table 4.5**. Each succeeding type of clue, **bolded in the sample prompt**, provides less direction, helping students to move toward "assistance-free" conceptual thinking.

Table 4.5. *Types of Clues and Sample Transitional Prompts*

Type of Clue	Sample Prompt
A list of terms to be included in the answer.	*Compare the rate of the water cycle in a desert to the rate in a tropical forest.* ***Be sure to include the terms solar energy, precipitation, evaporation, humidity and ground water in your answer.***
Reference to prior experience.	*Compare the rate of the water cycle in a desert to the rate in a tropical forest.* ***Think about the experiment we did with the water in the 2-liter bottles.***
Hints as to the type of terminology required for an acceptable answer.	*Compare the rate of the water cycle in a desert to the rate in a tropical forest.* ***Be sure to include contextually correct vocabulary terms from this unit.***

Source: Downing and Marquand (2000).

Another approach to the transition process is provided in the following examples of "common" assessment questions.

Common Assessment in Science: *Brian, all 72 kg of him, bungee-jumps from a 100-m tower toward the river below. He falls 35 m before the bungee cord starts to stretch. This cord can stretch 40% of its length and has a breaking strength of 7000 N.* <u>*When the bungee cord has reached its maximum length, does the tension exceed the cord's breaking strength?*</u>

Common Assessment in Math: *Draw a graph illustrating population growth that is doubling every ten years. Assume that the population in this* *current year is ten billion.* <u>If the environment can support a population with a maximum size of sixteen billion, in how many years will the population reach its maximum capacity?</u>

Common Assessment in Social Science: *The United States has a very diverse population. Some people consider this country to be a melting pot while others prefer the analogy of a pot of stew.* <u>Briefly explain each analogy. Which do you prefer and why?</u>

Common Assessment in Elementary Language Arts: *From the story we just read, make a numbered list of the key actions of the character you were assigned.* <u>Write the number of each action in the correct place on the plot graph you were given.</u>

Consider a ***transformed*** version of these problems, in which the <u>*underlined*</u> sentences are replaced by the following:

Science: *Will this become a "free fall" for Brian, or will he "bounce back"?*

Math: *Write a news release explaining why this year's graduating classes from local high schools don't need to worry about planning ten-year reunions.*

Social Science: *Write a letter to the editor in support of an "open door" or a "closed door" immigration policy for the United States. Use the idea of either a pot of stew or melting pot as the focus of your letter.*

Elementary Language Arts: *Make a character journal for your assigned character. You become the character. In the journal, explain why you acted the way you did (made the choices you did) for two of the key actions you listed.*

Several aspects of the transformed versions make them more effective for encouraging students to think rather than simply to look for the appropriate quantities to "plug in" to a formula. **Critical Thinking**, **Real World Tasks**, **Analysis**, **Synthesis**, and **Creativity** are all Learning Tasks that are incorporated into one or more of the transformed tasks.

The transformed version in science does not specify what must be calculated; therefore, it requires students to decide for themselves just what the problem is and how their knowledge of physics can be used to solve it.

You can help students learn to solve problems of this type by first providing them with a set of general questions, such as:

- How are the objects and situations in the problem similar to any objects or situations that were discussed in class? [Notice the reference to prior experience!]
- Which variables are already in content-specific terms and which can be converted to content-specific terms? [Notice the suggestion to consider past vocabulary!]
- Are all of the pieces of information in the problem relevant to its solution? [Including irrelevant information in a problem requires students to identify essential parts. If all the information in your questions or prompts is always needed, the implication to students is that everything is always important. By creating opportunities for your students to focus on "what's wrong with this prompt," you help them learn to discriminate between essential and non-essential information—a true-life thinking skill. (Based on Potts 1994, 2). We'll go into more depth in Chapter 6 concerning the benefits of determining what is extraneous information.]

It may sound strange to you, however, because of past experience, *many of your students come into your class with no understanding that assessment relates directly to course content.* Hints in transitional prompts help provide content-assessment connections. By starting a course with transitional prompts sprinkled among factual prompts, students will learn the expectations of an adequate answer to a conceptual prompt while achieving success during the learning experience. (*Recall the need for appropriate balance between challenge and support.*) They also begin to understand how your content fits into the "conceptual prompt framework" you are working towards. (*Recall DOK concepts here.*) As the course progresses, use of transitional prompts decreases—students are gradually weaned from the need for hints and clues. (*Recall ZPD, GRRM, and CBUPO concepts here.*)

Transitional prompts can be used for longer periods of time with students who are developmentally unprepared for conceptual prompts. (*Recall airplanes and bridges in **The Analogy**.*) In some classes, transitional assistance may be required only briefly in the beginning units of the course. (*If you have a lot of swimmers.*) In other classes, it might be appropriate for transitional prompts to be the predominant type prompt used in assessment for the entire course. (*Remember the Wise Advisor's caution about stopping all flights and bridge maintenance.*) In either case, or any case in-between, students are more challenged than they would have been by a steady diet of factual-only assessments.

You might be surprised. There will be students who became offended when assessed with too many factual prompts late in the semester or year. "What's the matter? You think we don't know this stuff, so you're asking only easy questions?" is a complaint we've heard. *And **that** is music to any teacher's ears.*

> Genius without Education is like Silver in the Mine.
>
> **– B. Franklin**

Answers to the Bloom/DOK/Verb Prompts

1. Describe four characteristics of _____ [**DOK 1**]
2. Describe how the events that led to World War I and World War II are alike and how they are different. [**DOK 3**]
3. Describe the most significant legislation for students with special needs and create a plan to evaluate compliance levels in your school district. [**DOK 4**]

References for Chapter 4

Anderson, Lorin W., and David R. Krathwohl, eds. 2001. *A Taxonomy for Learning, Teaching and Assessing: A Revision of Bloom's Taxonomy of Educational Objectives: Complete Edition.* New York: Longman.

Bloom, Benjamin S, M.B. Englehart, E.J: Furst, W.H. Hill, and David R. Krathwohls, eds. 1956. *Taxonomy of Educational Objectives: The Classification of Educational Goals, Handbook 1: Cognitive Domain.* New York: Longmans, Green.

Brim, Gilbert. 1992. *Ambition: How We Manage Success and Failure Throughout Our Lives.* USA: Basic Books a Division of HarperCollins Publishers.

Downing, Charles, and Marquand, Marilyn. 2000. "Tune up Your Teaching." Unpublished manuscript. Available online at http://www.engageinteaching.com.

Hess, Karin K. 2006a. "Applying Webb's Depth-of-Knowledge (DOK) Levels in Science." Accessed November 10. http://www.nciea.org/publications/DOKscience_KH08.pdf.

_____. 2006b. "Exploring Cognitive Demand in Instruction and Assessment." Accessed November 10. http://www.nciea.org/publications/DOK_ApplyingWebb_KH08.pdf.

_____. 2012. "A New Lens for Examining Cognitive Rigor in Assessments, Curriculum, & the Common Core: Connect the Dots: Implementing & Assessing the Common Core Standards." Presentation at Wisconsin ASCD Meeting, Madison, Wisconsin, January 11, 2012.

Hess, Karin K., Dennis Carlock, Ben Jones, and John R.Walkup. 2009. "What Exactly Do 'Fewer, Clearer, and Higher Standards' Really Look Like in the Classroom? Using a

Cognitive Rigor Matrix to Analyze Curriculum, Plan Lessons, and Implement Assessments." Presentation at CCSSO, Detroit, Michigan, June 2009.

Available online: http://www.nciea.org/cgi-bin/pubspage.cgi?sortby=pub_date

Hobbs, Nicholos. 1974. "A Natural History of an Idea." In *Teaching Children With Behavior Disorders*: Personal Perspectives, edited by J.M. Kaufman & C. D. Lewis, 145-167. Columbus, Ohio: Charles E. Merrill.

Krashen, Stephen D: 1982. *Principles and Practice in Second Language Acquisition*. Oxford: Pergamon.

_____. 2004. *The Power of Reading: Insights From the Research*. 2nd ed. Portsmouth, New Hampshire: Heinemann.

Potts, Bonnie. February 1994. "Strategies for Teaching Critical Thinking." ERIC/AE Digest. ERIC Clearinghouse on Assessment and Evaluation, Washington, DC. ED385606.

Strong, Richard W., Harvey F. Silver, and Matthew J: Perini. 2001. *Teaching What Matters Most: Standards and Strategies for Raising Student Achievement*. Alexandria, Virginia: Association of Supervision and Curriculum Development.

Sutman, Francis X, and Others. March 1993. "Teaching Science Effectively to Limited English Proficient Students." ERIC/CUE Digest, Number 87. ERIC Clearinghouse on Urban Education, New York, N.Y. ED357113.

Vygotsky, Lev S. 1978. *Mind in Society: The Development of Higher Psychological Processes*, edited by M. Cole, S. Scribner, V.J: Steiner, and E. Souberman. Cambridge, Massachusetts: Harvard University Press.

Webb, Norman L. 1997. Research Monograph Number 6: "Criteria for Alignment of Expectations and Assessments on Mathematics and Science Education." Washington, D:C.: Council of Chief State School Officers from the National Science Foundation.

_____. August 1999. Research Monograph No. 18: "Alignment of Science and Mathematics Standards and Assessments in Four States." Washington, D:C.: Council of Chief State School Officers from the National Science Foundation.

_____. 2002 "Depth-of-Knowledge Levels for Four Content Areas." Unpublished paper. March 28, 2002.

Webb, Norman L. and others. "Web Alignment Tool." 24 July 2005. Wisconsin Center of Educational Research. University of Wisconsin-Madison. 2 Feb. 2006. Accessed November 8. http://www.wcer.wisc.edu/WAT/index.aspx.

Webb, Norman L. 2009. "Webb's Depth of Knowledge Guide: Career and Technical Education Definitions." Available online: http://www.aps.edu/rda/documents/resources/Webbs_DOK_Guide.pdf.

Chapter 5

YOU CAN DO IT!
IMPLEMENTING SUCCESS
IN YOUR CLASSROOM

Chapter Overview - Responsibility Island

Today's students are a social group, often with a skewed concept of accountability. Here on **Responsibility Island**, you will learn about the importance of using "the social process" to your advantage and how to develop a Community of Practice in your classroom. Our last stop on this island tour is a look at how to put this all together and help you teach to the whole child.

A Quote to Kickstart Your Thinking

> Make my boat a speedboat! I have a short attention span—I don't have ADD, I just need to be engaged and entertained when I learn, and it has to be fast paced. If the process is slow and dull, I tune out. Well, your classes where ALWAYS entertaining, so I was engaged, even when I didn't want to be (when I was sleepy, would rather socialize,

etc.) In fact, for some activities we had to socialize, so it was perfect! [authors' emphasis] As a student, I almost could not help learning, despite my efforts to the contrary—and that's remarkable. If only more educators could do the same, how engaged would our children be? And armed with a lifelong love of learning? I can't help but think that children are born with an innate curiosity that the education system snuffs out.

Dr. CK-P: Doctor of Medicine

Introduction

"Once upon a time, there was a benevolent Monarch. She loved her subjects and they loved her." After all, *love is all you need.* If reciprocal affection *is* all that is needed for effective teaching and exceptional learning, we've all spent unnecessary time considering, studying and trying new methods, strategies, and programs to improve our practice. Time would have been better spent trying to figure out how to get our students to want a healthy relationship with us.

 Write down your thoughts about what you have just read.

Did you experience any internal pushback thinking we were dismissing the importance of the quality of the teacher/student relationship? Would your response be different if you taught a different population of students or a different grade level?

As we move the discussion from sentimentality to practicality, the influence of sentiment will be acknowledged. However, we'll expand it to include the overall quality of the social component of learning.

In Chapter 4, we emphasized three key concepts:

- the cognitive component of learning
- categorizing and leveling thinking
- learning as work

During the development of the concepts in that chapter, we stressed this part of our definition of learning: *A social process that requires **appropriate challenge** in terms of novelty, complexity, depth, and quantity.*

Our focus for this chapter shifts to the first part of that portion of the definition. The ***social process*** of learning assumes the prominent position in this chapter. Refer to **Figure 5.1** as you read the next paragraph.

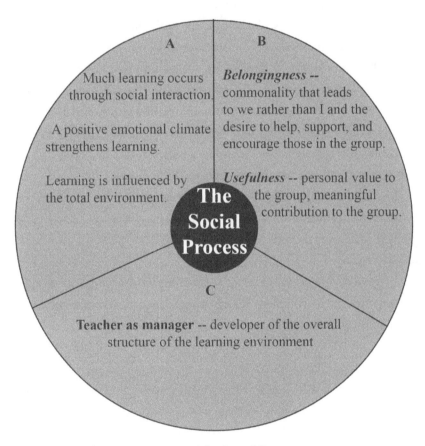

Figure 5.1: *The Social Process.*

Just How "Social" is the <u>Social</u> in Social Process?

In this chapter, we deliberate the synergistic condition created by interaction of the individual and the environment. Both the individual and the environment influence, change, and inform one another. Whether intentionally or by happenstance, this synergism will exist.

Ron Brandt, in his book *Powerful Learning* (1998), provides a list of research-based summary statements about learning that includes what is encapsulated in Sector **A** in **Figure 5.1**. Sector **B** summarizes some of Sagor's work. To complete the frame for the discussion on the social process of learning, we add one role of the teacher from Chapter 2 in Sector **C**. Finally, and "outside the box," we will consider what the phrase "teach to the whole child" should mean in your classroom.

Simply stated—we are social beings. The individual participates in a social world. That world includes both internal processes and the external context.

In 1990, the American Psychology Association first convened the Task Force, *Psychology in Education*. The task force was charged with conducting a meta-analysis of decades of research on learning, motivation, and development from the fields of psychology and education. They were presented with a formidable task of uncovering enduring principles and practices from both disciplines and identifying strong, authentic intersections.

The product of *Psychology in Education* was a document that presented a new paradigm for education: Learner-Centered Psychological Principles (APA 1993; 1997). This paradigm

> ... [provides] a framework for developing and incorporating the components of new designs for schooling. These principles emphasize the active and reflective nature of learning and learners
>
> (APA 1997).

This report was a "living" document—revisions would be made with new research and discoveries about learning, motivation, and developmental factors that affect learning.

The twelve principles pertaining to the learner and the learning process from the original 1993 report were expanded to fourteen principles in the 1997 version. The added factors were *learning and diversity* and *standards and assessment*. Contrary to the definition most commonly used in education, the term *learner* in Learner-Centered Psychological Principles includes *all stakeholders* involved with the educational system (students, teachers, administrators, parents, community members, etc.). The fourteen principles, taken holistically, provide a lens to view learners in real-world situations—not just in the classroom.[13]

> They [the fourteen principles] focus on psychological factors that are primarily internal to and under the control of the learner rather than conditioned habits or physiological factors. However, the principles also attempt to acknowledge external environment or contextual factors that interact with these internal factors
>
> (APA 1997).

The fourteen principles are grouped within four categories.

- Cognitive and Metacognitive Factors
- Motivational and Affective Factors
- Developmental and Social Factors
- Individual Differences

Table 5.1a. *Selected Learner-Centered Psychological Principles (a)*

Category/ Factors	Principle
Cognitive and Metacognitive #6 Context of Learning	• Learning does not occur in a vacuum • The classroom environment, particularly the degree to which it is nurturing or not, can also have significant impacts on student learning.

The tables (**5.1a-b**) above and below this paragraph provide details pulled from the categories that pertain to the social aspects of learning. Only two of the four categories are presented and the verbiage of the three principles presented was edited.

---

13 A link to the complete list of fourteen principles with short definitions is in **Resources** at the end of this book. A link to the full text of the Task Force report can be found on our website.

Table 5.1b. *Selected Learner-Centered Psychological Principles (b)*

Category/ Factors	Principle
#10 Developmental Influences on Learning	• Because individual development varies across intellectual, social, emotional, and physical domains, achievement in different instructional domains may also vary. • The cognitive, emotional, and social development of individual learners and how they interpret life experiences are affected by prior schooling, home, culture, and community factors.
#11 Social Influences on Learning	• Learning is influenced by social interactions, interpersonal relations, and communication with others. • Learning can be enhanced when the learner has an opportunity to interact and to collaborate with others on instructional tasks. • Learning settings that allow for social interactions, and that respect diversity, encourage flexible thinking and social competence. • In interactive and collaborative instructional contexts, individuals have an opportunity for perspective taking and reflective thinking that may lead to higher levels of cognitive, social, and moral development, as well as self-esteem. • Quality personal relationships that provide stability, trust, and caring can increase learners' sense of belonging, self-respect and self-acceptance, and provide a positive climate for learning. • Positive learning climates can also help to establish the context for healthier levels of thinking, feeling, and behaving. Such contexts help learners feel safe to share ideas, actively participate in the learning process, and create a learning community.

Source: Framework for School Reform & Redesign (American Psychological Association: Work Group of Educational Affairs, November, 1997).

The social environment of *school* includes more than who likes who, who gets along or doesn't get along with whom, what extracurricular activities are available, and how *we* as teachers prefer to configure our seating arrangements for individual or group work. When you restrict your definition of learning environment to the above, there will be problems. The research is conclusive—we are social beings and learning is influenced, enhanced, impacted, assisted, *and* encouraged by the quality of the social aspects of the teaching and learning environment.

 Defend the following statement: *The individual participates in a social world and that world includes both internal processes and the external context.*

We'll pause briefly and see how closely your thinking is aligning with ours.

"He Said/She Said"

Dr. D: I hope we're not implying that teachers need to create a "warm and fuzzy" classroom for learning to take place.

Dr. J: No, that's not the goal. *Warm and fuzzy* doesn't guarantee learning.

Dr. D: Well, I hope we're also not saying that teachers are responsible for making sure all students are friends and the classroom is a *happy* place where only smiles and high fives are welcomed.

Dr. J: And, once again the answer is, "No." It certainly might be easier to try to make students *happy*... no homework, no assessments, everyone gets an "A", no *hard* stuff to think about or do, etc. *Friends Only* allowed in my classroom. But that is far from the goal.

Dr. D: That's good to hear. If you have a classroom full of hormone embattled middle schoolers, *happiness* and *friends* change like the wind! Of course, the concept of happy and friend changes periodically in all grade levels—just faster and more frequently in middle school.

Dr. J: You're right about that. But that's not what we're talking about when referencing the social process and context for learning. We're talking about characteristics of a teaching/ thinking environment that inspire learning and provide the best conditions for achievement.

Dr. D: Sneaky. We're back to Essential Question #5.

Dr. J: Yes. But this time we're viewing the question from another perspective—the informed and intentional development of conditions for a learning environment that can result in it being considered a *community*.

Dr. D: Hold it! Let me lob you an easy pitch to hit out of the park. You wouldn't know of any theories or models that address this aspect of learning, would you?

Dr. J: Glad you asked. The answer is, "Yes." The model from social learning theory we'll investigate is *Community of Practice*, and our discussion begins... now!

Communities of Practice

The term *community of practice* originated with Etienne Wenger and Jean Lave. It stems from their significant contribution to learning theory—Situated Learning (Lave and Wenger 1991), where the focus was apprenticeships as a learning model.

People usually think of apprenticeship as a relationship between a student and a master. Studies of apprenticeship, however, reveal a more complex set of social relationships through which learning takes place. Most of the learning takes place between journeymen and more advanced apprentices. The term *community of practice* was coined to refer to the community that acts as a living curriculum for the apprentice (Wenger-Trayner 2011).

Lave and Wenger departed from traditional studies and perspectives of learning. They did not focus on the kinds of cognitive processes and conceptual structures involved in learning. They considered the kinds of social engagements that provide the proper context for learning. They argued that learning is a social process whereby knowledge is co-constructed in participation with others in community. Learning is situated in a specific context and particular social environment—it "… is the foundation of who we are (becoming). It is social because our human nature is social, not just because (or when) we interact with others or use certain tools" (Wenger 2012).

Wenger defines a community of practice (CoP) as

> …a group of people who **share** [authors' emphasis] a concern or a passion for something they do, [sic] and learn how to do it better as they interact regularly. This definition reflects the fundamentally social nature of human learning. It is very broad. It applies to a street gang, whose members learn how to survive in a hostile world, as well as a group of engineers who learn how to design better devices or a group of civil servants who seek to improve service to citizens
>
> (Wenger-Trayner 2011).

Based on the above definition, a classroom *can* also be defined as a CoP. The emphasis on the word *"can"* is not coincidental.

This is a "two-parter." Consider Wenger's definition of *community of practice*.
- Why is a classroom **not** automatically considered a CoP?
- Is your classroom a CoP? Defend your answer

There are three required structural elements in any type of CoP (Wenger 2011). The elements are a revision of Lave and Wenger's earlier collaborative and individual work. These elements are a *domain of knowledge*, a *notion of community*, and a *practice*.

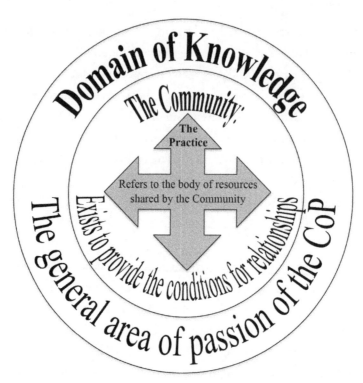

Figure 5.2. *Visual Depiction of Relationships*
Between the Community of Practice Concepts.

The **domain** of knowledge (general area of interest of the CoP) is the unifying and guiding component. It gives meaning to the activity of the members. Individuals are attracted to *and* inspired to participate and learn together, in community, to "…steward a domain of knowledge and to sustain learning about it" (Wenger 2011).

The **community** develops from a shared identity and *collective intention*. Not all community members have the same passion for the domain. That's okay, because the community exists to provide the appropriate conditions for joint activities, discussions, sharing of ideas, and building relationships. The community is established to foster collaborative and cooperative learning—learning that has value for each member. Community members participate at different levels of intensity and duration at different times. This is normal and expected of a healthy CoP as the community is *living*. Flexible boundaries for levels of involvement, degrees of engagement, and positions of authority are necessary.

The **practice** refers to the shared body of resources that exists as the result of committed engagement and contributions of individual members. According to Wenger, these resources result in a *shared repertoire* for the practice. Resources include experiences, individual stories, and strategies or methods to solve recurring problems. The resources and any *product* are available to all members of the CoP irrespective of their levels of involvement.

Whether you agree or disagree that compulsory education by default negates the possibility of a *community of practice* as defined by a *classroom*, please suspend any skepticism at this point. Consider the perspectives of *the members* of this particular social context—the classroom. To encourage your participation in this process, we've inserted another **STOP!** assignment.

1. Review Wenger's definition of a *community of practice*.
2. Review the three structural elements required.
3. Return to your response to the last STOP! and revise that response to include what would be required, from the perspective of *both* teacher and student, for the classroom to honestly be identified as a *community of practice*.

The level of integration of this revised answer into your pedagogical approach *will be a key determinant* in your success at developing independent thinkers in your classroom. **Table 5.2** provides eight summary statements about communities of practice.

In case you skipped the last **STOP!**, here's a shortened version of Wenger's definition: "A community of practice is a group of people who share a concern or a passion for something they do, and learn how to do it better as they interact regularly" (Wenger 2011). The underlying value of the CoP is *in the learning together*. Potential members of a CoP *may immediately see value* in coming together to begin learning with others of shared concern. When that occurs, they, commit to action. The *intensity* and *relevance* of the *value of learning* in relation to the **domain** (Wenger's general area of interest) in combination with the *nature of the relationships* influence how long the community of practice lasts. As a result, it *may take repeated and consistent practice of learning together before the value, and with it commitment to the community, is realized.*

Table 5.2. *Summary Statements about Communities of Practice*

CoP Summary
1. The process of learning and membership in a community of practice are inseparable. It is what lets us belong to and adjust our status in the group.
2. Communities develop around things that matter to people.
3. People organize their learning around the social communities to which they belong.
4. Knowledge is integrated in the life of communities that share values, beliefs, languages, and ways of doing things.
5. Real knowledge is integrated in the doing (the practice or ways of doing and approaching things that are shared to some significant extent among members), the social relations, and expertise of these communities.
6. A sense of joint identity and enterprise arises from organizing around particular activities and the general area of knowledge.
7. Members of a community of practice are involved in a set of relationships over time.
8. The interactions involved, and the ability to undertake larger or more complex activities and projects through cooperation, bind people together and help to facilitate relationships and trust.

Sources: (Ash 2010; Lave and Wenger 1991; Smith 2003; Wenger 2000).

When you first read the definition of a CoP, you may have thought, "Isn't this all an academic way of describing a *team or a task force... * people coming together to work on something and learning new ideas in the process?" Both groups assemble for a specific purpose and entail group involvement. Both also require an exchange of knowledge between members. In teams and taskforces, the depth and breadth of individual learning varies. Both rely on relationship development at the minimum for constructive cooperation. Although the differences may at first seem superficial or inconsequential, Wenger makes a point of differentiating between a CoP, a team, and a taskforce. **Table 5.3** summarizes his justification.

Table 5.3. *Comparing a CoP to a Team and a Task Force*

What?	Team
Why organized?	Complete a task
How long lasts?	Until task completed
Learning?	Members learn something in performance of task
Nature/value of relationships	• Learning does not define team; task does • Commitment & contributions to the task is main source of trust & cohesion among team
What?	**Task Force**
Why organized?	Address a specific problem often with broad or far-reaching scope
How long lasts?	Until report, recommendations, or plan of action developed
Learning?	May revisit progress on above periodically
Nature/value of relationships	• Members learn • Members usually selected based on applicable expertise & represent larger group or perspective • Analyze and form solution/plan of action • Commitment to the process of collaborative and cooperative work and those it represents—this serves as main source of trust & cohesion among team • Acknowledgement of other's expertise
What?	**Community of Practice**
Why organized?	Domain
How long lasts?	Varies based on intensity & relevance of value
Learning?	On-going learning via interactions sustains community

Nature/value of relationships	• Learning only occurs in relationship
	• Engaged as individual learner
	• Trust developed is the result of ability to learn together: to care about the domain, to respect each other as practitioners, to voice questions and challenges, and to provide responses that reflect practical experience
	• May accomplish tasks, but the tasks don't define the community

Your brain may be hurting a bit by now, so let's regroup. **First**, this chapter addressed learning as a social process and the related characteristics of a teaching/thinking environment that inspire learning and provide the best conditions for achievement. **Second**, theory and learning models that support the fundamental understanding of learning as *social* have been provided. This overview of theory and models provides you with a foundation for informed, purposeful, and practical actions that will transform your teaching and learning environment.

All this requires clarity about the implications for you, the teacher, or transformations will either never begin or they will stall before they are completed. To best support you on your transformational journey, we now investigate the implications of communities of practice for your teaching.

Implications of *Communities of Practice* for Teaching

"Educators should structure learning opportunities that embed knowledge in both work practices and social relations…" (Ash 2010). That is a pretty strong *should* and certainly easier said than done. The good news is, if you're reading this book, you are ready and willing to do the *hard work*. We'll help you move from "that's a nice idea, but…", or any similar thought, to "give me some steps to take." *Awareness* is step one for meaningful and lasting change.

> **Awareness #1**: Students *are* members of different communities of practice—attracted and committed to a domain (a learning need, an interest, a concern, a passion).

Awareness #2: Most CoPs are outside of a teacher's influence, but students do have experience as *practitioners* in their CoPs.

Awareness #3: Much learning can take place between the inexperienced and *more knowledgeable others* within **developed** social relationships. It is important to note that the "more knowledgeable other" *is not always* you, the teacher.

Awareness #4: Teachers take on the role of *manager* (this was part of the discussion in Chapter 4). As the manager, you develop the overall structure of the class environment. You provide appropriate and relevant learning opportunities. And, you **welcome** students' individual strengths and expertise to be tapped and infused in the setting.

As the classroom teacher, you **do** have the choice to take on the challenge of transforming the classroom to a learning environment that more closely embodies the characteristics of a CoP. The individual *ingredients* may already be present. Awareness is not sufficient to begin the process, however. Progressing from *awareness* to *reflection and analysis* is necessary. Begin by answering the following questions.

1. What is the *need* for the learning? In other words, what is the domain that students and you, the teacher, can agree upon that will sustain interest and commitment to learning together across time?

2. What is the *value* of learning together? This question requires a response that considers *value* from both you and your students' perspective. Remember, the *community* does not impose value; the value is birthed as an answer to shared value—the domain.

3. What are the *opportunities* for participation that are currently available to all members of your classroom (the potential CoP)? In other words, are the roles and responsibilities for you and your students fixed, or is there freedom to move across *boundaries*? Are you (teacher) always the expert and driving force for the learning and your students the novices and incidental participants? [Recall that much learning takes place between apprentice and journeyman.]

The questions above are for you to ponder as *first steps* in considering the implications of *communities of practice* on teaching *practice*. Before moving on, refer back to **Table 5.1** and **Table 5.2** and note the following phrases:

- interactive and collaborative instructional contexts
- quality personal relationships that provide stability, trust…
- process of learning and membership in a community of practice are inseparable
- a sense of joint identity and enterprise arises
- the interactions involved… bind people together and help to facilitate relationship and trust

A CoP cannot be established with a "one-way street" mentality of *what* should be valued, *who* is in charge of the learning, and *who* owns the product or resources generated from the shared learning. A CoP by definition is a "we."

As you begin to create a picture of what *is* and what *could be* in a transformed learning environment, keep in mind these two fundamental principles. A transformed learning environment (CoP)

1. Cultivates teachers and students who are compelled to interact, co-construct learning, and problem-solve while reaping the benefits of the shared repertoire of resources generated by the CoP
2. Generates life-long learners as evidenced by continuing interest in a topic or a learning need by means of participation as practitioners in learning communities beyond *school*

Transformation takes time. Intentional and purposeful choices and actions are required to develop a functioning *community of practice*. This requires a rethinking and re-orienting of teacher and student roles and an accurate understanding of the social principles of learning. Outside of school, students actively create or join communities to learn, practice, and produce resources and products for the benefit of the group as part of their normal routine. Unless your choices and actions integrate what students do naturally

This is the "world's longest **STOP!** assignment." But, if you do it all, you will have a really good start to implementing change in your classroom.

1. How would your classroom be different if your students considered themselves members and practitioners in a community (beginning with your classroom)?

2. How would relationships change within and between teacher and students if individual investment is respected and seen as essential to the health and effectiveness of the whole community?

3. How would instructional design change if learning value was a result of mutual engagement and trust developed from the ability to learn together?

Bottom lines:

4. What can you do to develop a classroom where students are willing to accept your vision of community?

5. What can you do to develop a classroom where students are committed to investing their own identities and become both practitioners and partners working to maintain the health and success of the CoP?

outside of school, transformation leading to formation of a community of practice is improbable.

Example of Transforming a Common Activity

Common Assignment in Any Core Area: *Use your textbook or notes to define the following terms. Give an example of each.*

    Social Science: *Teacher provided list of Forms of Government*

    Language Arts: *Teacher provided list of Literary Devices*

    Math: *Teacher provided list of Mathematical Functions*

    Science: *Teacher provided list of Parts of a Cell (Organelles)*

    Commentary: This assignment is completed as students look through their textbooks or notes. Definitions and examples are copied from either source and written on the student's paper with little regard to either context or importance.

In every discipline there are key concepts that are grouped together to form larger sets of information. Dictators, kings, and presidents are linked to various Forms of Government. Onomatopoeia and simile are two of many Literary Devices. Addition, subtraction, multiplication, etc., are grouped as Mathematical Functions. Cell Organelles make up cells. The list of such aggregations is very long.

In general, this is essentially a worksheet. Students find the information and fill in the definitions and examples on a form provided or their own notebook paper. Either way, **Engagement** is minimal. Depending on the situation, this might be a partner activity but is most commonly done in isolation.

Examples of the above as a Transformed Activity: *Catalogs*[14]

In this example of transformation, catalogs of student directions for the four content areas are provided. Teacher notes are specific to the **Science**: *Whole Cell Catalog*, but they provide basic requirements and expectations that apply to all the catalogs.

The Forms of Government Catalog

There's not much that you can't buy by mail order or online any more. There are catalogs for just about anything you can think of. Your task in this assignment is to create a catalog for something that there is not a market for yet... but you never know about the future. Your catalog will be for the major forms of government throughout history.

1. Form groups as instructed by your teacher.
2. Decide which individual in your group will be responsible for the catalog page (front and back or two fronts) describing each of the following forms of government.

---

14 These examples are available at Teachers Pay Teachers as individual products by discipline. In addition to the catalog, each product file also includes *individual* creative assignments in these content groups—résumés and classified ads. Ideas for scoring and peer grading/editing are part of each product. http://www.teacherspayteachers.com/Store/Chuck-Downing

Absolute Monarchy	Democracy	Democratic Republic
Dictatorship	Divine Rights Monarchy	Limited Monarchy
Oligarchy	Socialistic	Totalitarian Dictatorship

3. Use textbooks or other references to look up information on the form of government you were assigned. You may not cite Wikipedia as a reference in your catalog.

4. Design a page in your catalog for your form of government. Your page must include a word-processed description of your form of government and how it functions. You must include each of the following points and a reference number (3) where you explain each:
   A. Who is the Head of State?
   B. Who makes the governmental decisions?
   C. What the Source of Power is **and** how power is acquired and maintained?
   D. How long the Head of State rules **and** the process for replacing that Head of State?
   E. Who determines what political freedoms are granted?
   F. One other key piece of information on this form of government.

5. Your page must also contain the sales pitch, a contact name—and phone number, e-mail, and Twitter handle from an historical example of a leader of that form (e.g. Louis XIV) with the hourly rate(s) he charges as a consultant to those wanting to implement that form of government—and a full-color diagram to illustrate some aspect of your "form." Notes: **1)** Original art is preferred. However, if you download diagrams from the Internet or a CD-ROM: **a)** be sure to include appropriate reference citations. **b)** be aware that some diagrams are **big** files that might not print—try printing before the morning this assignment is due! **2)** All forms of government prices in your catalog should be comparable.

6. Be sure to leave a 1" margins on all edges.

7. Your group will need to design a cover for your catalog and produce a Table of Contents that will be the first page inside the cover of your catalog. The TOC should be done last. Use this format

Form of Government	Author	Page #	Points*
Absolute Monarchy	J: Student	1	
Democracy	Ima Kid	3	

Your instructor will fill in the "Points" column.

8. Your final grade on this assignment will combine your individual page grade with a "group" grade for the entire catalog.

This assignment will be graded on

Accuracy & completeness of description	**Neatness & how well you followed directions**	Creativity

The Catalog of Literary Elements

There's not much that you can't buy by mail order or online any more. There are catalogs for just about anything you can think of. Your task in this assignment is to create a catalog for something that there is not a market for yet… but you never know about the future. Your catalog will be for major literary elements.

1. Form groups as instructed by your teacher.
2. Decide which individual in your group will be responsible for the catalog page describing each of the following literary elements.

Alliteration	Analogy	Hyperbole
Irony	Metaphor	Onomatopoeia
Personification	Point of View	Simile

3. Use textbooks or other references to look up information on the literary element you were assigned.
4. Design a page in your catalog for your literary element. Your page must include a word-processed description of your literary device. You

must include each of the following points and a reference number (3) where you explain each:

A. A definition/description of the term and its usage.

B. One example of the term as used in one of the pieces of literature we have or are currently studying.

C. One original example of that device of your own.

D. One other piece of information you have located on this literary device.

5. Also part of your page is the sales pitch, a pricing structure, and a full-color diagram to illustrate your "device." Notes: **1**) Original art is preferred. However, if you download diagrams from the Internet or a CD-ROM: **a**) be sure to include appropriate reference citations. **b**) be aware that some diagrams are **big** files that might not print— try printing before the morning this assignment is due! **2**) All device prices in your catalog should be comparable.

6. Be sure to leave a 1" margins on all edges.

7. Your group will need to design a cover for your catalog and produce a Table of Contents that will be the first page inside the cover of your catalog. The TOC should be done last. Use this format

Literary Element	Author	Page #	Points*
Alliteration	J: Student	1	
Analogy	Ima Kid	3	

Your instructor will fill in the "Points" column.

8. Your final grade on this assignment will combine your individual page grade with a "group" grade for the entire catalog.

This assignment will be graded on

Accuracy & completeness of description	Neatness & how well you followed directions	Creativity

The Catalog of Mathematical Functions

There's not much that you can't buy by mail order or online any more. There are catalogs for just about anything you can think of. Your task in this assignment is to create a catalog for something that there is not a market for yet… but you never know about the future. Your catalog will be for important mathematical functions. A function relates an input to an output.

1. Form groups as instructed by your teacher.
2. Decide which individual in your group will be responsible for the catalog page describing each of the following functions

Addition	Area	Average
Circumference	Diameter	Division
Multiplication	Subtraction	Volume

3. Use textbooks or other references to look up information on the function you were assigned.
4. Design a page in your catalog for your function. Your page must include a word-processed description of your function. You must include each of the following points and a reference number (B) where you explain each:
   A. A definition of the function.
   B. One example of the use of that function in this class.
   C. One example of the use of that function in another area of mathematics.
   D. One other piece of information you have located on this function.
5. Your catalog page must also include the sales pitch, a pricing structure, and a full-color diagram to illustrate your "product." Notes: **1)** Original art is preferred. However, if you download diagrams from the Internet or a CD-ROM: **a)** be sure to include appropriate reference citations. **b)** be aware that some diagrams are **big** files that might not print—try printing before the morning this assignment is due! **2)** All function prices in your catalog should be comparable.

6. Be sure to leave a 1" margins on all edges.
7. Your group will need to design a cover for your catalog and produce a Table of Contents that will be the first page inside the cover of your catalog. The TOC should be done last. Use this format

Function	Author	Page #	Points*
Addition	J: Student	1	
Circumference	Ima Kid	3	

Your instructor will fill in the "Points" column.

8. Your final grade on this assignment will combine your individual page grade with a "group" grade for the entire catalog.

This assignment will be graded on

Accuracy & completeness of description	Neatness & how well you followed directions	Creativity

The Whole Cell Catalog

There's not much that you can't buy by mail order any more. There are catalogs for just about anything you can think of. Your task in this assignment is to create a catalog for something that there is not be a market for yet… but you never know about the future. Your catalog will be for the major organelles in a cell.

1. Form groups as instructed by your teacher.
2. Decide which individual in your group will be responsible for the catalog page describing each of the following organelles

Cell membrane	Mitochondria
Ribosome	Endoplasmic reticulum
Golgi apparatus	Cytoskeleton (flagella, cilia)

3. Use textbooks or other references to look up information on the organelle you were assigned.

4. Design a page in your catalog for your organelle. Your page must include a word-processed description of your organelle and its function. You must include each of the following points and a reference number (B) where you explain each:

    A. Definition of the term organelle.

    B. Description of the structure of the organelle.

    C. A list of products produced or processes involved.

    D. How your organelle interacts with at least one other organelle.

5. Your catalog page must include the sales pitch, a pricing structure, and a full-color diagram to illustrate your "product." <u>Notes</u>: **1)** Original art is preferred. However, if you download diagrams from the Internet or a CD-ROM: a) be sure to include appropriate reference citations. b) be aware that some diagrams are **big** files that might not print—try printing before the morning this assignment is due! **2)** All organelle prices in your catalog should be comparable.

6. Be sure to leave a 1" margins on all edges.

7. Your group will need to design a cover for your catalog and produce a Table of Contents that will be the first page inside the cover of your catalog. The TOC should be done last. Use this format

Organelle	Author	Page #	Points*
Cell Membrane	J: Student	1	
Mitochondria	Ima Kid	3	

Your instructor will fill in the "Points" column.

8. Your final grade on this assignment will combine your individual page grade with a "group" grade for the entire catalog.

This assignment will be graded on

Accuracy & completeness of description	**Neatness & how well you followed directions**	Creativity

Commentary: This catalog assignment increases the list of Learning Tasks dramatically. Production of the product is a moderately **Complex Task**. **Creativity** and **Engagement** at high levels are requisite. Ultimately, the final catalog is a **Synthesis** of many, many parts.

This particular example of Transformation is included here for a specific reason. This chapter has been a discussion of the social aspect of learning. Production of any of these catalogs requires significant, *productive* social interaction. As the former student remarked in the quote that opened this chapter, *"I was engaged, even when I didn't want to be (when I was sleepy, would rather socialize, etc.) **In fact, for some activities we had to socialize, so it was perfect!**"*

Even though your students won't know the theories behind your quality teaching, they will appreciate it.

Teacher notes: The Whole Cell Catalog

- You can use this idea for any content concept area that has "parts." For example in **Science**: Families of Elements; Types of Rocks; Simple Machines. In English/Language Arts: Parts of Text Structure. In Math: Geometric Formulas. In Social Science: Major Civilizations; Economic Systems.
- Model your "own" catalog project after these samples.
- Groups can be any size up to the number of categories (i.e., pages) to include. Two categories per student is not a burdensome load in most cases.
- Assign 30 points per page. Divide the 30 single-page points into three 10-point sub-units. 10 pts for the accuracy (I am merciless here.); 10 pts for the neatness and following of directions; 10 pts for the

creativity "sales pitch." Each student gets *x/30* for his/her page plus an additional amount based on the entire catalog (the Group Grade).
x/30 + group/30 = total/60

- **Group grade**: Average the scores for each page-including the cover (15 points) and table of contents (15 points) and add that to the individual score. Each group member gets the same group score added to whatever their page score was.

- **If one or more students do not turn in their pages on time, don't punish the whole group**. Change your "group grade" calculation by averaging only the scores of the pages turned in so the zeros don't bring down students who did their jobs.

- It's best if you assign the project and after 2-3 days have a group meeting time when all members share what they've accomplished so far. At that meeting, have them discuss possible prices so there is no big disparity between organelles.

- On the due date, give teams about 10 minutes to share and staple their catalogs together. I don't like folders because they are hard to stack.

Below is a sample rubric for scoring this item.
We like the rubric because…

- It shows the minimum expectations and specifically how to exceed them for additional credit.
- Kids have little room to complain.

We don't like the rubric because…

- You don't need a rubric. You can score this assigment with this checklist:
  Accuracy: 0 - 5 - 10
  Directions: 2 pts each for typing, full-color, description, sales pitch, pricing
  Creativity: 0-10

- **The rubric addresses more clearly the "Accuracy" category and clearly delineates expectations in "Directions" but is no more help on the creative piece than the checklist.**

- The group grade is not part of the rubric.

Rubric for The Whole Cell Catalog

Elements → Scale ↓	Element 1 Accuracy & completeness of description	Element 2 Neatness & how well you followed directions	Element 3 Creativity
(weights)	**33%**	**33%**	**33%**
4	Level 3 *plus* Description of organelle's function is referenced in the sales pitch.		Level 3 *plus* Reader is excited by the visual appearance **and** the writing on the page.
3	Level 2 *plus* All required components are described accurately.	Level 2 *plus* Sales pitch includes multiple reasons to buy. Pricing structure aligns with other pages.	Level 2 *plus* Reader is excited by the visual appearance **or** the writing on the page.
2	Description of organelle's function is accurate. All required components are addressed.	Word-processed. Sales pitch. Price included. Full-color diagram - original art or referenced. Correct margins	Form matches other pages in the group.
1	Did not meet **all** Level 2 Requirements.	Did not meet **all** Level 2 Requirements.	Did not meet **all** Level 2 Requirements.

You can use this rubric as a "model" for scoring any catalog assignment you assign. Be sure to provide access to the rubric from the beginning of the assignment—students/groups need to be aware of the expectations from the start of any assignment. No rubric "gives away" answers—the rubric simply defines the scoring parameters.

Provide each group with one of your rubrics and have them "self score" their catalog on the due date. Place the self-scored copy in the final catalog. If you use a different color from that of the students when you grade, it will provide a clear visual of "why did we only get…"

You can use Sample Peer Grading Sheet for a Botany Catalog as a model for scoring any catalog assignment you assign. It is a table in MSWord (7 columns by 31 rows. Times New Roman font. Mostly 8 point [kids have good eyes], but titles are in 10 point **bold**.). The full size version of this is also in each of the Teacher Pay Teacher products described in the footnote.

Teaching to the Whole Child[15]

Earlier in this chapter (**Figure 5.1** *The Social Process*), we referred to *teaching to the whole child*. It can easily become one of "those phrases"—overused until it becomes a cliché. We want *you* to consider recapturing the original and meaningful intent—to commit to a teaching and learning environment that honors the whole individual while *you* study, prepare for, and implement instruction that takes into consideration the influences of these *parts*.

In Chapter 1, we stated that learning as a whole is composed of several processes:

- a *social* process
- a *mental* process
- a *perceptual* process
- a *collaborative* process

---

15   Authors' note: This book does not address a spiritual dimension of *wholeness*. It is not our intent to be dismissive of this dimension. This component requires a careful and in-depth treatment that is beyond the scope of this project. For a thought-provoking glimpse into this dimension, you may want to consider Rachael Kessler's book, *The Soul of Education: Helping Students Find Connection, Compassion, and Character at School* published by ASCD.

Sample Peer Grading Sheet for a Botany Catalog

PreAP Biology: Botany Catalogue Peer Scoring Table – *Place this inside the catalogue it was used with.*

PRINTED Group Members (alphabetical! Last, First):

	10	8	6	4	2	0	
Cover:							
Looks like catalogue	10	8	6	4	2	0	
Neat	10	8	6	4	2	0	
Colorful	10	8	6	4	2	0	
TOC:							
All member's names on it	10					0	
Pages in correct order (based on directions)	10					0	
Page numbers included				10 (all)	5 (some)	0	
Total for Cover and TOC							**/60**
Each Individual Page:							
Flower: *Accuracy:* at least one fact checked in book	10		6	4	2	0	**Page total:**
Following Directions: sales pitch, title, price, picture (if not original, citation included) [2@ - 10 if all]	10		6	4	2	0	
Creativity: Color, looks like other pages, neatness, "coolness" [2@ - 10 if all]	10		6	4	2	0	
Fruit: *Accuracy:* at least one fact checked in book	10		6	4	2	0	**Page total:**
Following Directions: sales pitch, title, price, picture (if not original, citation included) [2@ - 10 if all]	10		6	4	2	0	
Creativity: Color, looks like other pages, neatness, "coolness" [2@ - 10 if all]	10		6	4	2	0	
Leaf: *Accuracy:* at least one fact checked in book	10		6	4	2	0	**Page total:**
Following Directions: sales pitch, title, price, picture (if not original, citation included) [2@ - 10 if all]	10		6	4	2	0	
Creativity: Color, looks like other pages, neatness, "coolness" [2@ - 10 if all]	10		6	4	2	0	
Root: *Accuracy:* at least one fact checked in book	10		6	4	2	0	**Page total:**
Following Directions: sales pitch, title, price, picture (if not original, citation included) [2@ - 10 if all]	10		6	4	2	0	
Creativity: Color, looks like other pages, neatness, "coolness" [2@ - 10 if all]	10		6	4	2	0	
Seed: *Accuracy:* at least one fact checked in book	10		6	4	2	0	**Page total:**
Following Directions: sales pitch, title, price, picture (if not original, citation included) [2@ - 10 if all]	10		6	4	2	0	
Creativity: Color, looks like other pages, neatness, "coolness" [2@ - 10 if all]	10		6	4	2	0	
Stem: *Accuracy:* at least one fact checked in book	10		6	4	2	0	**Page total:**
Following Directions: sales pitch, title, price, picture (if not original, citation included) [2@ - 10 if all]	10		6	4	2	0	
Creativity: Color, looks like other pages, neatness, "coolness" [2@ - 10 if all]	10		6	4	2	0	
Total from Peer Review (all pages + cover/TOC)							**/180** / (150 if only 5 pages)

Checkpoints: #1, #2.

Reviewers Names:

We emphasized that strategic teacher and student choices and behaviors, when intentionally connected, set up conditions for movement from passive to active learning *and* *teacher-dependent* **to** *student-independent learning.* Integration of the processes is necessary for effective learning.

Collaborative process. Different roles for teacher and student and varying levels of control were discussed in Chapter **2**—recall the Gradual Release of Responsibility Model. Successful navigation through the GRRM levels requires the development of healthy relationships, trust, and respect *for* and *between* teacher and student. The *collaborative* dimension is an essential part of effective teaching.

Perceptual process. The *personal and affective* components of the *whole child*—your students—took center stage in Chapter **3**. We explored the importance of the interaction of personal goals, emotional arousal processes, and personal agency beliefs. Proper perceptions are *vital* to a successful learning environment.

Mental process. Chapter **4** focused on the *cognitive* aspects of teaching and learning. There is a balance of challenge and support, quality of cognitive rigor, and categorizing and leveling thinking that is critical in an effective teaching environment. *Balance* in this setting requires knowledge and understanding of the personal and affective components— both *mental* processes.

Social process. We completed our discussion of *teaching to the whole child* with this chapter (**5**)—the social dimension that is inseparable from all. We are *social* beings… period.

References for Chapter 5

American Psychological Association Task Force on Psychology in Education. January 1993. "Learner-centered Psychological Principles: Guidelines for School Redesign and Reform." Washington, DC: American Psychological Association and Mid-Continent Regional Educational Laboratory.

American Psychological Association. November 1997. "Learner-Centered Psychological Principles: A Framework for School Reform & Redesign." Prepared by the Learner-Centered Principles Work Group of the American Psychological Association's Board of Educational Affairs (BEA).

Ash, Doris. 2010. "Summary of Learning Theories-Cal Teach Program." ED 230 F2010 Reader. Accessed September 15, 2013. calteach.ucsc.edu/courses/.../Summary%20of%20*Learning*%20Theories.

Brandt, Ron. 1998. *Powerful Learning*. Alexandria, Virginia: Association for Supervision and Curriculum Development.

Kessler, Rachael. 2000. *The Soul of Education: Helping Students Find Connection, Compassion, and Character at School*. Alexandria, Virginia: Association for Supervision and Curriculum Development.

Lave, Jean, and Etienne Wenger. 1991. "*Situated Learning. Legitimate Peripheral Participation*." Cambridge: University of Cambridge Press.

Smith, Mark K. 2003. " 'Jean Lave, Etienne Wenger and Communities of Practice,' The Encyclopedia of Informal Education." Accessed October 8, 2013. www.infed.org/biblio/communities_of_practice.htm.

Wenger, Etienne. 2000. *Communities of Practice: Learning, Meaning, and Identity*. Cambridge University Press.

Wenger-Trayner Website [Beverly Wenger-Trayner & Etienne Wenger-Trayner]. "Intro to Communities of Practice." Last modified 2011. http://wenger-trayner.com/theory/.

_____. "Communities Versus Networks?" Last modified Posted by Team BE Dec. 28, 2011. http://wenger-trayner.com/resources/communities-versus-networks/.

_____. "What is a Community of Practice?" Last modified Posted by Team BE Dec. 28, 2011. http://wenger-trayner.com/resources/what-is-a-community-of-practice/.

_____. "What is Social Learning?" Last modified Posted by Team BE January 1, 2012. http://wenger-trayner.com/all/what-is-social-learning/.

Chapter 6

TRAINING WHEELS HAVE VALUE, BUT THEY'RE IN THE WAY IF YOU KNOW HOW TO RIDE A BIKE.

HOW TO KNOW WHEN TO TAKE THE TRAINING WHEELS OFF

Chapter Overview - Perseverance Island

So your students don't want to keep on trying until they come up with an answer. That's happened to all of us at some time. Here on **Perseverance Island**, Chapter 6, we'll look at some examples of why "keeping on keeping on" is a vital part of the learning process. You'll investigate the ideas of moving from novice to journeyman to expert and what that movement entails. Here's where you'll find out why practice doesn't always make perfect, and look at a surprising study on the efficacy of mental practice.

A Quote to Kickstart Your Thinking

> *It was not until I finished high school that I really realized what I had had in your class. I just remember thinking things like how difficult you were and how it was SO important to follow every little instruction. Now in retrospect I think of so much more... those two years made a big difference!*
>
> **MT**: Lewis and Clark University.

Introduction

> *What we hope ever to do with ease, we must learn first to do with diligence.*
>
> Samuel Johnson

The chances are good that you've seen it—probably more than once. The scene is a castle. An old sorcerer trudges from his lair. Then, a figure enters through the door. The small black body with plate-sized ears and a whip-like tail is immediately recognizable. When the figure pulls the sorcerer's hat down over his ears and begins to direct the mops and buckets to do his bidding, you know disaster is only a few musical measures away.

Of course, we're referring to Disney's *Sorcerer's Apprentice* segment of the classic animated feature, *Fantasia*. As you suspected, the sorcerer (expert/master) must rescue the apprentice from his doom. As we go through this chapter, discussing the novice to expert/master continuum model, please keep an open mind. Our *goal* is for *your* students to *avoid* Mickey Mouse's fate. We want you to know how to provide a pathway from novice to expert/master that gives you and your students the best chance of a successful ending.

The brief quote by Samuel Johnson that helps open this chapter is one of those statements that we all know to be true. But it is one we tend to forget as the internal and external pressures to *perform* exceed the reality of our current levels of competence and experience. You might wish that the *diligence* component was unnecessary and that *ease* was the defining factor. However, neither you nor your students can reach *ease* without persistent effort, informed practice, and context-based experience.

An aside—actually what might be going on *inside your mind* right now...

It's the first paragraph of this chapter, and I am already feeling tired! I'm supposed to work on improving critical thinking, motivation, social learning, transform activities... **where do I start?!**

Fear not! Here's the answer:

Start where you are!

Begin your process in the same way you'll determine the starting point for your students when planning and preparing for *their* transition to the *ease* that Samuel Johnson refers to.

In a perfect world, all students would enter your classroom with the requisite skills and knowledge to move smoothly down the road to the targets you set for them. They would all move at the same pace and in the same direction...

And back to reality...

Back also to Chapter 2 and the *heart of the teacher*—your reasons for entering the profession. Recall we said that the heart of the teacher includes the commitment to "do good", to help, to nurture, to challenge for growth—to be resolute in finding ways to make content come alive and cultivate students who are excited about learning.

So, take a deep breath; realize you're not alone in this; and let's move forward. We'll help you begin to consider how *you* can reach the *ease* Samuel Johnson referred to and what type of learning environment is necessary to allow *your students* to do the same.

Essential Question #6 is a good place to start our discussion. *What does the teacher need to continue to do, and what does the teacher need to do differently?* In other words, what changes are needed in *your thinking and doing* to become the Monarch described in paragraph **XXXII** of **The Analogy**?

And then the Monarch truly understood the words of the Wise Advisor. She saw that her subjects were much better subjects as she allowed them more freedom in how and where they traveled. In fact, she came to realize that the greatest gift she had given them was the freedom to explore and then appreciate their efforts, because they were successful at hard work. The resultant rewards her subjects received were much more valuable to them because of her willingness to empower them to do things on their own.

Both the Monarch and the subjects made changes in their thinking, their choices, and their behavior before they arrived at *understanding, empowerment,* and *competence (*aka ***ease)***. This chapter addresses topics that illuminate the path of that process.

Novice to Master Continuum

> The top experts in the world are ardent students. The day you stop learning, you're definitely not an expert.
>
> **Brendon Burchard**

We live in a culture where hyperbole is commonplace. *Icon, diva, expert,* and *master* are labels that today carry only a faint resemblance to their original meaning. Unfortunately, some educational trends and practices have added to the diminution of qualities or characteristics that are compulsory if someone is to attain such distinctions as *expert* and *master.*

Grade point averages above 4.0, the "easy A," "everyone gets a trophy," and assessment methods that establish mastery as percentage correct combine to muddy the waters of meaning of the terms expert and master. There's also a perception that the designation of *novice* is undesirable—a label to be quickly shed rather than to accept as an essential part of the natural rhythm of learning.

Grant Wiggins puts this in perspective in his article "How Good Is Good Enough?" (2013/14):

> Knowing that you're a novice who's a long way from true mastery is not inherently debilitating. On the contrary, having a worthy, far-off goal and tracking your progress in closing the gap are key to mastery in all walks of life. (15)

There are different models that describe levels of practitioner knowledge and skill development. All of these mental models are simplified representations of a complex process. There are differences in the number of steps in those models. The descriptors of those steps differ as well. Regardless of the model, crucial to any attempt to Tune up Your Teaching is knowing when "show or tell me" is appropriate and when "to get out of the way!"

There is on-going debate as to which model best represents both the "know how" [implicit knowledge] and "know that" [explicit knowledge]. Adding to this milieu, neuroscientists continue studies on brain functionality as it relates to the localization and specialization of processing these different ways of knowing. Important work continues into the nature and degree of interaction between implicit and explicit knowledge, especially as it relates to *expert*.[16]

For the purposes of this book, we accept that there are different ways to group attributes representing knowledge and skill development. What we present is a practical and reasonable continuum that was synthesized from multiple models.

But first a bit of a history lesson—back to the *Middle Ages*. The short story that follows traces the development of an apprentice to a master. Interspersed are portions of **Table 6.1** that provide the name of the stage in our model and attributes associated with that stage.

Bronislav's Story

The sun poked its feeble rays through the early grey sky. Bronislav pulled his trousers up, pushed his feet into his shoes and headed down to the workshop. Even though he had not lived with the Master long, he knew better than to waste time before arriving to begin his day's work. When the workday began, Bronislav knew at least twelve hours would pass before it ended.

As he entered the workshop, the Master spoke without looking at him. Bronislav moved to the Master's shoulder and carefully observed. The Master described each individual step he performed in the production of the piece he was working on. Specific information was burned into Bronislav's mind. Only

---

16   For further study, review theory on explicit and implicit knowledge from the following sources found in References: Polanyi, M. (1966) and Sun R, Matthews C., and Lane, S (2007).

occasionally was he allowed to handle any of the materials involved in the process—so scarce and valuable were they that the Master carefully rationed them throughout construction.

As Bronislav climbed wearily into bed that night, he breathed a prayer of thanks. He knew how fortunate he was to be apprentice to this Master.

Table 6.1a. *Attributes of the Novice/Apprentice Stage*

Novice/Apprentice Stage
• new to or inexperienced in a situation or field
• emotions engaged (fear, concern about mistakes, need for validation)
• wants rules, specific guidelines
• little experience in context/real-life situations
• difficulty determining what is important
• patterns not evident
• needs close monitoring via instructional feedback & structured self-observation/reflection
• "Just tell me what to do."

Months passed. Bronislav became more and more competent at his assigned tasks. Occasionally, the Master would allow him to organize materials. It was a rare occasion when he was allowed to participate in the production of the Master's product.

Finally, the day came when the Master told Bronislav to get out a second set of materials. His heart swelled with pride as the Master moved a bench adjacent to his own. He was instructed to begin work and follow his Master's lead.

That night as Bronislav climbed into bed, he was a different kind of tired. Overriding any fatigue was his awareness that he had achieved the next stage— he was beginning the next chapter in his journey. This night he prayed that one-day he could be a *master* that was as respected as his own.

Years passed. Bronislav increased his knowledge and skills under the tutelage of the Master. Finally, a day came when the Master was waiting for *him* as he entered the workshop.

Table 6.1b. *Attributes of the Competent/Initial Stage of Journeyman*

Competent/Initial Stage of Journeyman
• able: having enough skill or ability to do something
• performs to basic standards
• adequate
• begins to notice patterns
• still more "rule-driven" than conceptual
• needs increasing opportunity to practice/experience real situations (in context)
• can identify/recognize specific examples/instances
• needs increasing variety in terms of novel situations and problem-solving to further develop
• "How am I doing?" Partner with Me—You take the lead

"Help me move this," the Master gravely directed. He indicated the table Bronislav had been using with a gesture. Bronislav quickly moved to the end of the table opposite his mentor.

"This belongs in front of the south facing window. You require space of your own."

Together, the two men relocated Bronislav's workstation some distance across the room from the Master's table.

"I've been commissioned for more pieces than I can produce in the time given. You will make some of those without my help."

As the Master turned back to *his* workstation, he thought, *I pray he is ready for this responsibility.*

Buoyed in spirit by this vote of confidence, Bronislav set to work on the first of his assigned pieces of the Master's commission. Over the ensuing months and with decreasing frequency, the Master checked on Bronislav's progress. For his part, after a time, Bronislav rarely realized when the Master stood behind him. His focus was a mental picture of the piece that would truly represent *his* knowledge, skill, and creativity.

Solutions to problems came more and more easily as his prior experience and deliberate practice became second nature. *His* piece continued to take

Table 6.1c. *Attributes of the Proficient/Developed Stage of Journeyman*

Proficient/Developed Stage of Journeyman
• high degree or skill in something
• whole situations have meaning—more than just discrete bits or aspects
• actions/performance/choices relevant to long-term goals
• aspects more or less important depending on relevance to goal
• uses learned principles to determine relevance to goal
• experience different authentic situations
• growing repertoire of situations, reactions, solutions
• appropriateness of response/action
• can change perspective or action based on changing situation
• can vary performance based on unique situations
• needs access to resources and more sophisticated examples/models/ situations (in context/real-life)
• increasingly personal learning and connection to performance
• "This is what I am doing." Partner with Me—I'll take the lead

shape and fulfill *his* mental vision and expectations. *His* careful planning was manifesting itself. *He* began to wonder if this might be *his* masterpiece.

Unfortunately, when the Patron received the pieces commissioned to his Master, Bronislav learned that his *masterpiece* was not among them. His discouragement passed, however, as the Master assigned him more of his commissioned pieces. Bronislav was well aware that the road ending in **his own shop** was long and arduous.

Bronislav's thirtieth birthday passed unnoticed by anyone but himself. However, later in the month of his birth, he entered the workshop and found himself alone. He was unconcerned—this happened occasionally when the Master was out seeking new commissions.

Bronislav, now a *proficient/developed journeyman*, began work on his assigned piece that would complete the set he had been crafting. So absorbed was he in the work that he was unaware when the Master returned that day. The Master waited until an appropriate time in the production of the piece.

Then he placed a hand on Bronislav's shoulder. As the journeyman turned, he realized that two other masters were present.

"Arrange your pieces on my table. I have associates who wish to examine them."

Bronislav couldn't be sure, but he thought the Master's voice was tinged with just a hint of pride. After arranging his pieces as instructed, Bronislav stepped away from the table. He watched with nervous expectancy as the three masters handled, examined, and discussed his pieces and his workmanship. It was at least an hour before any of them even glanced his way. When they did, it was not his Master who spoke.

"Your master speaks highly of your discipline and skill. We now need to hear the kind of man you are."

Table 6.1d. *Attributes of the Expert/Master Stage*

Expert/Master Stage
• vast experience in different situations
• appropriate choices and actions driven by integration of honed analytical skills, deep reflection, accurate critique
• facility to look ahead and predict/anticipate
• characterized by collegial dialogue, sharing of experiences
• self-initiating, proactive in seeking information, solutions
• exemplifies constructivist learning
• performance appears intuitive
• performance appears to be improvisational
• consistent ability to eliminate distractors and irrelevant information for the specific situation
• creative
• inventive
• absorbed in performance
• "Let me teach you."

Sources: Dreyfus and Dreyfus 1980; 1986; Benner 1982; Daley 1999; Rosenberg 2012; Wiggins 2013/14; Tomlinson 2013/14.

After a time spent questioning his devotion, his honesty, and his family, he was dismissed from the room. He, his wife, and two small children watched from the window of his upstairs room as the two visiting masters left. Moments later, the door to his room opened. His Master stepped in.

"I have news. First, I will soon have need of this room. I am adding a new apprentice."

"Is there other news, Master?" Bronislav felt his heart pounding as he fought the nervous tremble in his throat.

"Only this. The guild welcomes you, Bronislav, as its newest member. The commission on your **masterpieces** will be enough for you to establish your own workshop."

The categories in **Table 6.1** don't have rigid boundaries. There is blurring when one is close to moving to the next level. It's also possible for the same individual to be in different levels at the same time, based on specific knowledge, skill sets, and experience. For example, one of your students might be very skilled (a *master*) at narrative writing but struggling with expository writing (a *novice*), or an *expert* at using mathematical formulas but struggling with their real-life applications (a *novice*).

 We don't often use a **STOP!** and have you go back to **The Analogy**, but for this **STOP!** we're asking you to do just that. Look for examples of how the subjects of the kingdom moved along a novice to expert (apprentice to master) continuum.
1. What was available or not available to them along the way?
2. What if any changes did you find in opportunities, perspectives, or perceptions of all concerned?
3. Did the materials that were available make a difference?
4. What part did the *Monarch* play in this process?

Figure 6.1 illustrates the changes that occur at the different levels in our continuum (Benner 1982). Feel free to return to your answers and modify as you see fit after comparing your ideas to the figure.

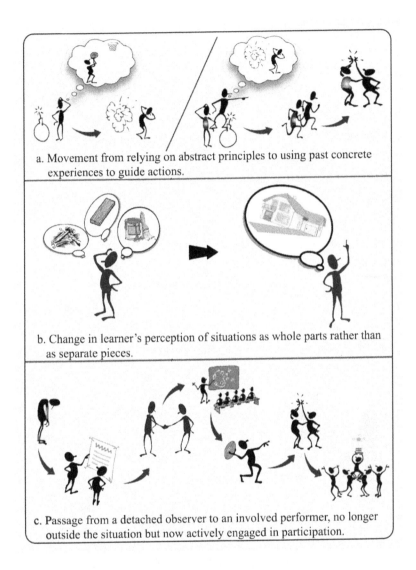

a. Movement from relying on abstract principles to using past concrete experiences to guide actions.

b. Change in learner's perception of situations as whole parts rather than as separate pieces.

c. Passage from a detached observer to an involved performer, no longer outside the situation but now actively engaged in participation.

Figure 6.1. *Changes in Learners by Level of Mastery.*

Focus on the Expert/Master Level

To become a master at any skill, it takes the total effort of your: [sic] heart, mind, and soul working together in tandem.

Maurice Young

There is evidence that experts use two modes of thinking: analytic (hypothetic–deductive) and non-analytic (pattern recognition)... Both modes of thinking are part of a continuous process.

Adolfo Pena

The two introductory quotes eliminate the perception that expertise is simply an intellectual process. Hopefully, by this time in your reading, it is apparent that we subscribe to the principle that learning is a complex process and engages more than the intellect.

Mastery also implies attitudes that characterize success—a work ethic, willingness to think strategically, tolerance for ambiguity, capacity to delay gratification, clarity of what quality looks like...

(Tomlinson 2013/2014).

Research indicates that an individual must internalize and take action in four areas to achieve expert/master level. These areas are:

- an identification with a specific and *meaningful* goal or pursuit
- an *accurate* self-awareness of current levels of knowledge and skill as they *relate* to the ideal or target goals/performance
- a *desire* to persistently engage in the hard work required to conquer obstacles
- a commitment to *achieve* at optimal levels

If you take another look at **Table 6.1d**, you'll notice the term "intuitive" in the descriptor of expert/master. There is debate as to whether or not an appropriate action or wise decision (*intuitive thinking*) overrides the presupposed knowledge and skills that allow for *intuition*. When considering the type of learning that must take place to transition from novice to expert/master, a definition that includes untaught or innate is *invalid*. What appears to be intuitive or instinctive for the expert/master is actually evidence of an informed, experience-based, and highly specialized response.

Early in Chapter 3, we defined *flow* as a spontaneous and effortless experience achieved when there is a close match between a high level of challenge and the skills needed to meet the challenge.

> True intuitive expertise is learned from prolonged experience with good feedback on mistakes.
>
> **Daniel Kahneman** - Nobel prize-winning psychologist

Attaining expert/master status also necessitates *paying dues* at the lower levels. In other words, the *master* has gone through at least three essential processes.

- trial and error
- accepting directed and then leveled support
- accumulating a repertoire of meaningful and practical strategies and solutions to inform next steps

Trial and error learning is critical.

> An expert is someone who knows some of the worst mistakes that can be made in his subject, and how to avoid them.
>
> **Werner Heisenberg**

Learners must have multiple opportunities to practice, have the time to practice, and be supported by formative feedback. Recall Bronislav, the apprentice, who worked under the watchful and committed "eye" of his master. He sought opportunities to demonstrate improvement over time. The master knew what the **end goal** was and that there were no shortcuts in the developmental process. A master's *role* is to provide an environment where each trial and error event is authentic and fuels both a reflective and a feedback/corrective process. There must be clarity by both the master and apprentice as to what constitutes excellence.

Consider the conditions necessary for movement along the continuum from novice to expert/master.

1. How much opportunity do you provide in your teaching and learning environment so both you and your students can accomplish the "...effective and graceful transfer of learning to meet authentic challenges" (Wiggins 2013/2014)?

    A. In other words, what are you doing to become a master?

    B. How often do you provide chances for your students to move along the same continuum?

We admit that was a soul-searching **STOP!** So, let's lower the affective filter and lower the stress level. What have you read in this chapter that informs an answer to **Essential Question #6**? *What does the teacher need to continue to do, and what does the teacher need to do differently?* In other words, "What changes are needed in your thinking and doing to become the Monarch described in paragraph **XXXII** of **The Analogy**?"

Since Practice Doesn't Necessarily Make Perfect, <u>What Type of Practice is Needed</u>?

> Practice is the master of all things.
>
> **Caesar**

One common characteristic in the four stages described in the novice to master continuum is *relevant practice in context*. This implies engagement and learning in authentic experiences. The learner takes on the identity of *practitioner* (recall Chapter 5 and importance of the practitioner identity). While simulations and other de-contextualized experiences may be practical and necessary in the beginning, at some point, the ***real*** has to be experienced if the *expert* or *master* label is to be achieved.

Practice is defined as doing something repeatedly in order to improve. A familiar saying is *practice makes perfect*.

1. Do you believe that?
2. What is your definition of *perfect*?
3. Does what is being *practiced* make a difference in the definition? In other words, do you consider practice for a sport's skill to be fundamentally different from practice for an *academic* skill such as writing an expository paragraph?

We understand that ongoing work in neuroscience will, maybe sooner than later, relegate what is now "current" and "accurate" to other categories. But in order to help you answer the above questions and understand the value of practice, we will look at some research that answers the question: What happens in the brain during *practice*?

Research studies have been conducted with musicians, non-musicians, and medical students. These studies focused on three things: *factors that influence* mental practice, *different types* of practice, and *sleep* in learning and practice (Pascual-Leone et al. 1995; Walker and Stickhold 2005; Ericcson 2006). Sleep is very important both in memory formation and in filtering the "white noise" from neural connections formed during practice. Our discussion now focuses on the first two factors.

The brain is an amazing organ—it looks for patterns, seeks efficiency, and makes new connections with the least provocation. It does not discriminate between *right* and *wrong* as it merrily responds to repeated *messages* with the creation of new synapses. At the neuronal level, "correct practice" is subjective. New synapses are formed in response to whatever input is provided.

In order to become more efficient, your brain makes connections between its different parts. The good news...the brain seeks to make connections and strengthen those connections with repeated messages (think *practice*). The bad news...the brain seeks to make connections and strengthens those connections with repeated messages (think *practice*). Our brains undergo change with every new learning attempt.

When incorrect, wrong, erroneous, irrelevant, or off-target *messages* are sent, two things must occur for correction:

1. strengthening groups of synapses so the *right messages* can be passed on
2. weakening another group of synapses that is relaying *wrong messages*

That's twice the *work*.

With continued learning, new synapses are formed between previously *unconnected* neurons. Groups of neurons (neuronal ensembles) work in concert to make message sending more efficient, accurate, and organized. Consider a newly formed soccer team. Initial practice sessions will include many individual mistakes and only a resemblance of what the actual performance should look like. This is like the initial activity of neuronal ensembles.

With accurate and timely feedback, consistent and appropriate practice, and continued clarity as to the desired final outcome, individual mistakes will decrease and a *team* will emerge. Subsequently, the following three components of "team play" appear to happen automatically: movement in concert, anticipated next steps, and seamless execution of skills. The skillfully functioning team is the picture of neuronal ensembles that have developed over time to produce streamlined, cohesive, and intelligible messages (Gebrian 2010).

 Think back to your response to the following question (posed at the beginning of this section): Do you believe that practice makes perfect? Explain how your response changed as a result of any new understandings.

Deliberate Practice

Elite performers, researchers say, must engage in 'deliberate practice'—sustained, mindful efforts to develop the full range of abilities that success requires. You have to work at what you're not good at.

Atul Gawande

Deliberate practice towards *expert* is not limited to performing a skill over and over again. According to K. Anders Ericsson (2006), a pioneer in research on *deliberate practice*, an expert also deconstructs complex tasks to specific skills. The expert then chooses which skills to focus practice on—those that need improvement.

Timely feedback is a companion to accurate self-analysis of performance. Necessary, also, is an increase in the level of challenge associated with the skill set being developed. A critical component is the individual's intent, commitment, and desire to actually master what is being practiced.

The preceding paragraphs should remind you of previous information. For example, *increasing the level of challenge* is analogous to i+1 in Chapter 3. The concluding sentence in the second paragraph relates to the concept of self-efficacy and motivation discussed in Chapter 4.

A study conducted with 875 first through third year medical students focused on the role of deliberate practice in the acquisition of clinical skills and the novice to expert continuum (Duvivier et al. 2011). The relationship between the years as a medical student, deliberate practice, and clinical skill test results was studied. The researchers were looking at identifying study habits related to deliberate practice.

Researchers identified the following four factors or aspects of deliberate practice that resulted from data analysis:

1. planning
2. concentration/dedication
3. repetition/revision
4. study style/self-reflection

Student scores on the importance and type of planning increased over time. Student scores on improvement of clinical skills due to repetition/revision were not sustained after year one. This result makes sense since, across time, automaticity of certain routine tasks/basic skill sets, while practiced, would not yield additional improvement.

Additional results of the study showed increases in

- concentration/dedication with respect to practicing
- focus on the tasks at hand

- awareness of desired outcomes
- a tendency to structure work

While gradually refining performance, "…it appears that students gradually learn how to make more efficient use of their time, energy and resources. In short, they seem to learn how to learn" (Duvivier 2011).

To expand on Duvivier, in short, students and teachers were responsible for specific essential ingredients that led to improvement. One student ingredient was establishment of clear purposes and goals. The second student ingredient was the development of the motivation to do well *and* improve. One teacher ingredient was carefully crafting learning opportunities designed to provide practice to overcome identified weaknesses. The second teacher ingredient was providing specific informative feedback.

Mental Practicing

It is unfortunate that you and your students will not always have the proper resources, time, space, or other circumstances conducive to providing authentic and sustained practice. Stay encouraged—there is a way to provide your students with meaningful opportunities to hone their knowledge and skills. It even works for complex tasks.

A study conducted for the National Institutes of Health (Pascual-Leone et al. 1995) yielded *thought-provoking* results. Non-musicians were divided into two groups. Each group was assigned a keyboard scale to practice with their right hand only for two hours a day for five days. The catch… one group could only practice mentally. Specifically, they were not allowed to move their fingers during this mental practice. The only time their fingers touched the keyboard was during testing at the end of each day.

After five days, a total of ten hours of actual practice on the keyboard, the physical practice group was able to play the scale perfectly. The *mental practice* group, when tested at the end of the five days, was able to play at the same level of the physical practice group at their three day mark. The *mental practice* group was then given two hours of physical practice time on the keyboard. They were able to match the performance level of the ten-hour physical practice group after only two hours of actual physical practice!

UNPRACTICED

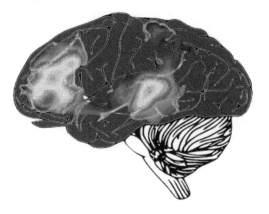

PRACTICED

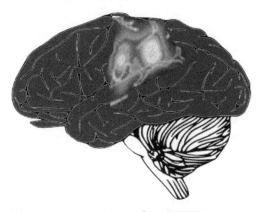

In this composite of a PET scan and a line art image of a brain, lighter colors indicate increasingly higher levels of brain activity in that region.

Figure 6.2. *Pet Scan of the Brain of a Person Before and After Practicing a Skill. While not specifically a brain that was using mental practice, the scan shows how different parts of your brain are involved at different times in any skill-based situation.*

The results of this study do not imply that mental practice is all that is needed. Instead, it suggests that mental practice, as a supplement to physical practice, can be an important factor in successfully reaching goals and attaining increased levels of mastery. The brain *is* making the correct connections during this mental practice.

Practicing is an art, just as much as performing is, and practicing intelligently and in ways that derive the maximum benefit from our brains' natural abilities will only serve to enhance our artistry as [_____ fill in the blank—authors' addition]

(Gebrian 2010)

Thinking as a practitioner—that is the key.

"He Said/She Said"

Dr. D: I don't know how to break this to you, but most of the teachers reading this book won't have the same students for 20 years. How are they going to work this novice to expert continuum thing?

Dr. J: They only have to work on pieces of the continuum. The key is that they know their students' starting places.

Dr. D: How can they know that?

Dr. J: Diagnostic and consistent formative assessment.

Dr. D: Sounds familiar. How will they know what to look for when they do assess?

Dr. J: Here's a good place to start. The novice wants rules and specific guidelines. Teachers may notice that the student is not recognizing patterns that seem obvious. Often everything involved in a situation may seem equally important to the novice—the ability to discern the importance of elements or pieces of information frequently escapes them.

Dr. D: Oh! Have I got a deal for *you*. The two transformed activities that follow both require students to distinguish essential from extraneous materials in that activity.

Dr. J: That's great. It will give teachers a starting point and help them develop *purposeful and effective creative thinkers*.

Dr. D: Seems like I've heard part of your answer before... Anyway, the activities do require students to think like an *expert*.

Dr. J: And, how do you know that?

Dr. D: Because I read the list of attributes in Table 6.1d.

Dr. J: Glad you're paying attention. I'll bet all of our readers read it, too.

Dr. D: [rolls his eyes]

Example of Transforming an Activity

One of the most under-emphasized aspects of teaching is providing opportunities for your student to learn what issues or materials are required when solving a problem. Most of the problems given to students in primary grades provide the necessary requirements for obtaining the desired solution using the preferred methodology. While this is a time-tested way to teach problem solving, it is severely lacking as a methodology for thinking—outside the classroom problems rarely arrive with only what's necessary for their solution attached.

This example of transforming an activity includes two distinct tasks—each containing extraneous items in their lists of materials. "Have a (Golf) Ball" requires specific content knowledge in math and/or science; the other activity is content neutral. Any time you have a project for students to complete, you can add extraneous materials. Just be sure you include the phrase, "your group can have access to (but do not necessarily have to use)" in the title "Materials."

Here are unembellished examples of how to include extraneous materials in social science and language arts.

- In a geography class, you might provide a political map of an area as a choice for students to use when asking for topographic features—the political map is extraneous.

- In a language arts class, if students are working on one genre of story, your materials' list might include an item from another genre as the extraneous item.

The activities that follow are designed to emphasize **Analysis, Complex Tasks, Creativity, Curiosity, Engagement, Persistence**, and **Real World Tasks** of the Learning Tasks listed in Chapter 1. While these specific activities should not be the only examples of determining extraneous information in your class, they do offer creative ideas for encouraging such discrimination in thinking of solutions to problems of any type.

Support Your Local Text Books
(Any Content Area)
An Open-ended, Problem-solving Activity

Problem:

How do you support two (2) or more big, thick textbooks (like a science, math, or social science text, or an anthology) 2.5cm/1 inch off the top of your table?

Materials your group can have access to (but do not necessarily have to use):

8.5 x 11" paper	(1 sheet)	Scotch tape	(4"/10cm strip)
Scissors	(1 pair)	6"/15 cm ruler	(1)
Pencil or pen	(1)	Sealable baggie	(1)

Parameters:
1. Form groups as instructed by your teacher.
2. Take one piece of notebook paper. Title this paper "grade sheet" and write down all your group member's names on it.
3. You can try as many times as you like, but each attempt using new paper and tape must be recorded by your teacher on your "grade sheet."
4. The books must be 2.5 cm off the tabletop for enough time to be measured by the teacher.

5. 2.5 cm is defined as between 2.3 cm and 2.7 cm. **1-inch** is defined as between 7/8 and 1-1/8 of an inch.

6. The books must be level. All four corners must be within the height limitation.

7. Successful support of 2 books with an "original plan" qualifies for 100% credit.

8. Successful support of 2 books with a plan "borrowed" from another group qualifies for 90% credit.

9. *Additional credit can be earned for additional books supported by an "original" plan. (5% per book up to 150% maximum)*

Questions: Answer only those questions assigned to you by your teacher.

1. Describe how you used each item on the materials list in your solution to this problem.

2. What was the maximum number of books supported by any group in your class?

3. How many books did your design support?

4. Compare your design to the "best in the class."
   A. How were the two designs similar?
   B. Why do you think that the "best in the class" design was *the best*?

Teacher Notes for Support Your Local Textbook

- Depending on the solution devised by a group, the pen or pencil, the tape, the sealable baggie, and/or the scissors may be deemed extraneous by that group. The most effective solution we've seen (described below) has no use for the baggie, and might not require the pen or pencil.

- The "grade sheet" is a 1/2 sheet of used paper with the names of the two students who worked together on it.

- Give out one piece of paper to each team at the beginning of the exercise. You may choose to provide a new sheet of paper and strip of tape for each trial by a group.

- You dispense the tape, or you'll end up with a lot less tape at the end of this activity.

- Mark "Attempt #" with some annotation each time a group comes to you for more paper or tape. This is how you know if they end up "borrowing" another idea for supporting the books.

- Use scratch paper for this activity—there's no sense in wasting good paper on this.

- "Original" means that the group thought up the solution independently. It does not mean unique.

- After the first group (or groups) solves this problem, other groups may choose to "borrow" their idea. If you have been monitoring the activity, you will be able to tell when that happens.

- A creative group can support up to 30 heavy science books with these materials. Actually more could be supported, but the stack becomes unmanageable after 30 books, or fewer, depending on the quality of the book's binding and the ability of students to reach the top of the stack.

- In our experience, the most effective solution to this problem involves cutting the paper into 1-inch (2.5cm) strips. Taping two or three of those strips into one long strip and rolling the long strip into a tight "pillar" provides very strong support. Five such pillars, placed near each corner and the center of the bottom book will support an inordinate number of books.

- We know of at least a half-dozen other strategies that will provide a viable solution to the problem.

- If you do this in multiple periods of students, do whatever you can to swear each class to secrecy. You want your last class of students to be just as challenged as your first class.

- Cut a piece of cardstock into a rectangular "measuring tool" that is the maximum height the books can be off the table to receive credit. Cut a notch out of one end at the minimum height. As long as the minimum height end of the measuring tool *will fit* beneath the bottom book on each side, and the maximum height end *will not fit* under the bottom book, that group has solved the problem.

Have a (Golf) Ball
(Math/Science)
An Open-ended, Problem-solving Activity

Problem:

Determine the volume of a golf ball.

Materials you have access to (but do not necessarily have to use):

Graduated cylinder	(1)	Scale/Balance	(1)
Scissors	(1 pair)	6"/15 cm ruler	(1)
Beaker or cup	(1)	Water	(as needed)

Parameters:

1. Form groups as instructed by your teacher.
2. Obtain a golf ball from your teacher. *If the golf ball hits the floor (or another student) during this activity, your grade goes in the tank!*
3. Design a procedure to determine the volume of the golf ball.
4. Write down your group's procedure on one piece of notebook paper with the names of all group members on it.
5. Take the paper with your group procedure on it to your teacher for her/his signature.
6. Perform your procedure and record your results on your paper and on the "common" space as directed by your teacher.
7. Modify your procedure if necessary.
8. Perform the procedure again and record your results on your paper and on the "common" space as directed by your teacher.
9. Turn in your group's paper.

Questions: Answer only those questions assigned to you by your teacher.

1. Describe how you used each item on the materials' list in your solution to this problem.
2. Did every group get the same volume for their golf ball? Explain your answer.

3. How would your procedure have been different if you would have been calculating the volume of a marble and not a golf ball?

4. Convert your calculated volume to liters.

5. The formula for density is mass/volume. What is the density of your golf ball?

6. Write down a brief procedure for determining the volume of a Styrofoam ball. (Hint: Styrofoam floats.)

Teacher Notes for Have a (Golf) Ball:

- Provide a space on your whiteboard or on your projection system for recording the calculated volumes. Without this class data, students cannot answer question #2.

- If you use graduated cylinders, make sure they have a diameter that is smaller than the diameter of the golf ball or the task is very simple.

- Students choosing the "scientific" method of determining volume do not need the ruler or the string. A common "scientific" solution is to use the graduated cylinder to measure the amount of water needed to fill the beaker or cup to the brim. Carefully place the golf ball in the beaker and use the graduated cylinder to measure the water remaining in the beaker or cup. The difference in the two volumes is the volume of the golf ball.

- Students choosing a "mathematical" solution, do not need the cylinder, beaker, or water. If a group uses the string to measure the circumference of the golf ball, they can calculate the radius of the ball. Using their calculated value of the radius, they can use the formula for volume of a sphere to calculate the answer.

- There is no valid reason to use the balance in this activity. It is "extraneous," unless you assign question #2. Even then, it is not required to determine the volume of the golf ball.

- Step #5 allows you to check on the use of "the little gray cells" by your students so you can begin to track their thought processes. You can just stamp any paper that has a *followable* procedure on it. The criterion for acceptance is whether another group could do what was written down without any outside explanation. Alternatively, you can ask leading questions to any group whose procedure has flaws and allow them to correct those flaws before they begin.

The student quote at the beginning of the chapter probably made little sense when you read it. After reading this chapter and considering "...following every little instruction" and "...two years..." of experience making a difference to that student.

What have you learned about the novice to expert/ master continuum that helps align his thinking with the continuum? Make a bulleted list of key points.

FYI. The quoted student has achieved the expert/master level in the field of graphic design as evidenced by his client list, which includes Nike.

References for Chapter 6

Benner, Patricia. 1982. "From Novice to Expert". *American Journal of Nursing*. 82(3): 402-407.

Daley, Barbara J: 1999. "Novice to Expert: How Do Professionals Learn?" Adult Education Quarterly 49(4): 133-147.

Dreyfus, Stuart, and Hubert L. Dreyfus. 1980. "A Five-Stage Model of the Mental Activities Involved in Directed Skill Acquisition." Supported by the Air Force Office of Scientific Research (AFSC), USAF, under Contract F49620-79-C-0063 with the University of California, Berkeley. Unpublished study. February 1980.

_____. 1986. *Mind Over Machine: The Power of Human Intuition and Expertise in the Era of the Computer*. New York: The Free Press.

Duvivier, Robert J:, Jan van Dalen, Arno M. Muijtjens, Véronique Moulaert, Cees van der Vieuten, and Albert Scherpbier. 2011. "The Role of Deliberate Practice in the Acquisition of Clinical Skills." *BMC Medical Education* 11: 101.

Ericsson, K. Anders, Neil Charness, Paul J: Feltovich, and Robert R. Hoffman, eds. 2006. *The Cambridge Handbook of Expertise and Expert Performance*. Part of Cambridge Handbooks in Psychology.

Gawande, Atul. 2011. "Coaching a Surgeon: What Makes Top Performers Better: Personal Best." *The New Yorker: Annals of Medicine*: 9-16.

Gebrian Molly. 2010. "What Musicians Can Learn about Practicing from Current Brain Research." Accessed November 10, 2013. http://madisonjazz.files.wordpress.com/2010/05/ practicingandcurrentbrainresearchbygebrian.pdf

Pascual-Leone, Alvaro, Dang Nguyet, Leonardo G. Cohen, Joaquim P. Brasil-Neto, Angel Cammarota, and Mark Hallett. 1995. "Modulation of Muscle Responses Evoked by Transcranial Magnetic Stimulation During the Acquisition of Fine Motor Skills." *Journal of Neurophysiology* 74(3):1037-1045.

Pena, Adolfo. June 2010. "The Dreyfus Model of Clinical Problem-Solving Skills Acquisition: A Critical Perspective." *Medical Education Online 2010*; 15:10.3402/meo.v15i0.4846. doi: 10.3402/meo.v15i0.4846.

Polanyi, M. (1966). *The Tacit Dimension*. Univeristy of Chicago Press.

Rosenberg, Marc. 2012. "Beyond Competency: It's the Journey to Mastery that Counts." *Learning Solutions Magazine.* Accessed November 15, 2013.

http://www.learningsolutionsmag.com/articles/930/beyond-competence-its-the-journey-to-mastery-that-counts.

Sun, R., Robert C. Matthews, and Sean M. Lane (2007). "Implicit and Explicit Processes in the Development of Cognitive Skills: A Theoretical Interpretation With Some Practical Implications for Science Instruction. In Elizabeth M. Vargios ed., *Educational Psychology Research*:1-26. New York: Nova Science Publishers.

Tomlinson, Carol Ann. 2013/2014. "Let's Not Dilute Mastery." *Educational Leadership* 71(4): 88-89.

Walker, Matthew P., and Robert Stickgold. 2005. "It's Practice, with Sleep, that Makes Perfect: Implications of Sleep-Dependent Learning and Plasticity for Skill Performance." *Clin Sports Med* 24: 301-317. This work was supported by grants from the National Institutes of Health (MH 48,832, MH 65,292, MH 69,935, and MH 67,754) and the National Science Foundation (BCS-0121953).

Wiggins, Grant. 2013/2014. "How Good is Good Enough?" *Educational Leadership* 71(4): 10-16.

Chapter 7

LET GO AND ENJOY!
REAPING THE BENEFITS OF
<u>ENGAGING IN THINKING</u>

Chapter Overview

Even though there are no more islands, that doesn't mean it's the end of your journey. Outside of the transformation process of the common activities, we didn't talk about integration of information from multiple islands. Remember, this isn't a recipe book—it's a map you can use on your professional journey of integration. In this chapter, our goal is that you will see there is value to being part of a group at times—even if you're the type of independent spirit who prefers solitary professional development. In this chapter, we present rationale for becoming part of a group of like-minded practitioners and invite you to join the Community of Practice we've established via our website.

A Quote to Kickstart Your Thinking

> ...[W]e had your typical power point lectures, tests, and reading assignments but those aren't the things I remember. I vividly

remember spitting into a petri dish to test the acidity of my saliva, lining up as Thymine in a DNA molecule to practice the replicating processes of DNA, and more than anything... dissecting the pig. These engaging hands-on experiences allowed me to learn in such a way that would last a lifetime, not just until I finished my final. There are not many other classes I've taken, even in college, that I can say will withstand the tests of time and leave me with knowledge that would carry me through many successes in the future, but the ways in which Dr. Downing taught me to explore, enjoy, and appreciate knowledge through creative, hands-on learning experiences will take me not only through my final quarter of college, but through many accomplishments to come!

AC - University of California, San Diego

Let's Regroup

The title of this book encourages you to **Tune Up Your Teaching** so you can **Turn On Student Learning** in whatever educational situation you find yourself. You've placed yourself somewhere along the educator's novice to expert continuum through your analysis of **The Analogy** and your answers to our **STOP!** questions along with your implementation of different strategies and models we've presented. This chapter is designed to validate your efforts. For that reason the title of this chapter includes a directive, an invitation, and a promise.

Let Go...of any expectation, self- or other-imposed, that you need to change everything you've done, and do it right now. That is not only self-defeating, it's unrealistic. Start with one area of the teaching and learning process to examine closely and take action to move from what has been *common* in your practice to *transformed*.

Enjoy... the process of questioning the status quo of how "school" is done and challenging yourself to choose a new vantage point from which to view teacher roles and student roles. The alternative is begrudging the policies and trends that seem to only "pile" more work on rather than make any meaningful and substantive change.

Reap the Benefits... of witnessing your students grow in competence and confidence as you develop and sustain a learning environment that requires engaged, creative, and critical thinkers—inquisitors and problem-solvers who seek collaboration and challenge.

Reap the Benefits... of taking on the identity of *student* again as you expand your professional repertoire and revitalize your practice through questioning, examining, analyzing, and experimenting.

Please have your answers to the first six **Essential Questions** handy. You'll want to review them as you read this chapter.

Essential Questions from a Different Perspective

We opened the book with **Essential Question #1**: What is learning? And as we near the end of the book, we now ask you to consider **Essential Question #7**: *What basics about teaching and learning do I need to consider as valuable for renewed study, professional reflection, and discussion?* In between those two **Essential Questions** were others that asked for a response from a particular perspective—the "I", the "we", or the "student voice."

Let's revisit two of the **Essential Questions** from a different perspective. In Chapter 2, we introduced **Essential Question #4**: *What is the target? When students leave my classroom, they will be_____.*

That was a question that we asked you to consider as you progressed through the book. Now, consider a revision of the question: *What is the target? When my teaching career is over, I will have been a teacher who was_____ and who did_____.*

Were you able to come up with specific qualities or characteristics for each blank that could be observed and measured? Alternately, did you discover that your thinking resulted in more of a general narrative or philosophical explanation? By the way, we are not going to provide you with a *right* response, as there is no one right response. The more specifics in your response though, the greater the chances you will be able to formulate a plan to fulfill your self-portrayal.

Chapter 4 addressed qualities of a *thinking environment* that would inspire and provide the best conditions for achievement. For example, the balance of challenge and support was emphasized and **Essential Question**

#5 was introduced: *What type of thinking environment is necessary to reach the target? A thinking environment that is_____.*

You considered the influence of learning as work, just manageable difficulties, categorizing and leveling thinking, and cognitive rigor from the perspective of the impact on your students. Now, consider another perspective as you react to the following revision of **Essential Question #5**: *From **my** (that's you) perspective, what type of thinking environment do **I** need to achieve the professional target(s) **I** have set for myself? In other words, what type of thinking environment do **I** need in order to realize **my** answer to the revised **Essential Question #4** and hit **my** target?*

Here is our final **STOP!** for you. It is the last of our **Essential Questions** and focuses on you—the teacher. No matter what point on the novice to expert continuum you currently place yourself, the hallmark of a life-long learner is willingness to wonder and to see things anew.

Set aside enough *uncluttered* time to write a response to **Essential Question #7.** *Then write your answer.* Your response may serve as the impetus for action research or for joining other professionals who are similarly motivated to delve deeper into their teaching practices.

Essential Question #7: *What "basics" about teaching and learning do I need to consider as **valuable** for renewed study, professional reflection, and discussion?*

Teaching and Reflective Practice

At the beginning of this book, we told you that we acknowledged your experience and expertise and purposefully would not talk "down" to you as we presented information and ideas. We hope you feel we've honored that commitment up to now. We know that this topic has the potential to push one of your buttons. What we include here is designed to help you **Tune Up Your Teaching**—nothing more.

Part of the definition of learning presented in Chapter 1 is that learning is a mental process. This process requires the development of metacognition or the monitoring of understanding, awareness of the need for assistance or correction, and the ability to recognize and effectively employ cognitive strategies.

We also stated in Chapter 1 that we were committed to providing you with an opportunity to hone your skills as a reflective practitioner through both professional self-study and collaborative discourse with colleagues. In this section, we are encouraging you to tap into your experience and expertise as you review, refine, and revitalize your craft as an educator.

> Few activities are more powerful for professional learning than reflection on practice.
>
> **Charlotte Danielson** and **Thomas McGreal**

Reflection has been viewed as a superficial and almost leisure activity—a passing fad in professional circles. Reflection can also be viewed as a disciplined process that is:

1. **Systematic**: regular, organized, efficient, logical
2. **Deliberate**: thoughtful, intentional
3. **Sustained**: persistent

The second view more closely characterizes what is termed *reflective practice*. One objective of reflective practice is developing a quality of reflection that allows for reproducibility of successes. *Effective* reflective practice recognizes serendipitous occurrences and the unexpected "ah ha" moments that help to shape new understandings and ways of addressing both content and pedagogy.

You have probably surmised that there is not one definition for reflective practice. Nuances exist within the same discipline and differences exist between disciplines. If you review the writings of Dewey (1933), you'll find reference and explanation of the relationship between reflection (a specialized type of thinking) and learning by doing, i.e., practice.

In an article titled "Reflecting on 'Reflective Practice'" (2008), Linda Finlay provides a synthesized definition of reflective practice: the process of

learning through and from experience towards gaining **new insights** of self and/or practice. This process requires questioning.

1. *Why* am I doing *what* I am doing in the *way* I am doing it?
2. What benefits might there be for an alternative approach to the content, situation, or problem?
3. What did I learn?
4. What did my students learn?

Reflective practice theory is often attributed to Donald Schon as outlined in his influential publication *The Reflective Practitioner: How Professionals Think in Action* (1983).

He dissected reflective practice into two types of reflection:

- **Reflection <u>in</u> action**. This type of reflection is *thinking while doing*. The practitioner may be faced with the element of surprise or an unexpected event or situation. This causes a pause and a regrouping or shifting in originally intended action. The reflective practitioner in action seeks to understand the unique situation as it is while recognizing the repertoire of examples, models, and experiences already held.

Schon explains it this way:

When a practitioner sees a new situation as some element of his repertoire, he gets a new way of seeing it and a new possibility for action in it, but the adequacy and utility of his new view must still be discovered in action. Reflection in action necessarily involves experiment... This *experimenting* involves exploration, taking action to produce an intended change, and succeeding at discriminating between competing hypotheses [a tentative explanation for the situation/problem that needs further investigation]

(Schon 1983, 141 &147).

- **Reflection <u>on</u> action**. This type of reflection is *after the doing*. The practitioner asks questions such as:

1. Why did I do what I did?
2. What happened during the lesson or activity?
3. What do I need to know or be able to do to improve my practice?

The practitioner engaged in *reflection on action* undertakes the process that is most commonly understood as *reflection*. This is a critical look backwards and is focused on an analysis and evaluation of past practice for the purpose of future improved practice.

Killion and Todnem (1991) added this third way of reflecting.

- **Reflection <u>for</u> action**. This type of reflection combines both *reflection in action* and *reflection on action*. *Reflection for action* is characterized by an examination of both past and present actions. The reflective practitioner sets specific guidelines and a plan of action to succeed in the given task in the future. Requirements for *reflection for action* are summarized in **Table 7.1**.

Table 7.1: *Requirements of Reflection For Action*

Task analysis	Self-motivation beliefs
• goal setting	• self-efficacy
• strategic planning	• outcome expectations
	• intrinsic interest/value
	• goal orientation

All three of the types of reflection are profitable for the nature of change in the teaching and learning environment we advocate in this book. While there are a number of different models for teaching and reflective practice, each having strengths and weaknesses and each having advocates and critics, the bottom line is...

When teachers engage in reflective practice, they improve their teaching effectiveness, leading to increased student performance

(Chase et al. 2001).

Schon (1983) helps to frame a distinction of the reflective practitioner as one who is

> ...presumed to know, *but I am not the only one in the situation to have relevant and important knowledge. My uncertainties may be a source of learning for me and for them* [authors' emphasis] (300).

Opportunity Costs of Transformation

> Excellence is never an accident. It is always the result of high intention, sincere effort, and intelligent execution; it represents the wise choice of many alternatives –choice, not chance, determines your destiny.
>
> **Aristotle**

For a choice to be a choice there must be an alternative. What is chosen has a cost in terms of what wasn't chosen—the opportunity cost. In other words, what you have to give up by choosing one thing over the other is the opportunity cost. Choices certainly would be easier to make if the outcome or consequences were certain. Unfortunately, that is not how it works. *Straddling* options also does not work. You *must* choose one or the other.

Richard Elmore (2008; 2009) states there are basically three ways to increase student learning and school performance throughout our educational system:

1. Raise the **level of content** [*rigor* – authors' wording] that students are taught
2. Increase **teacher knowledge and skill** brought to the teaching of the content
3. Increase the **level of students' active learning** of the content

According to Elmore, if you want to realize improvement in student learning, a change in the first element necessitates a change in the other two.

The teacher, the student, and the content are interdependent components of what Elmore defines as the *instructional core*.

> If you alter the content without changing the skill and knowledge of teachers, you're asking teachers to teach to a level they can't – they don't have the skill and knowledge to teach to. If you do either one of those things without changing the role of the student in the instructional process, the likelihood that students will ever take control of their learning is pretty remote.
>
> (Elmore 2009).

Consider the above statement in terms of opportunity costs. We learn to *do* the work by *doing* the work. We don't learn by telling other people to do the work, and we don't learn by hiring experts to do the work. [authors' modification of Principle Number Six] (Seven Principles of the Instructional Core from Elmore 2008). In other words, you have to make the choices and accept the affiliated opportunity costs.

This book is about *choices*. Throughout, we have asked and prodded and challenged you to make *choices*. The unspoken core question you may have asked yourself several times during your journey with us is, "What am I sacrificing?" Perhaps you expanded the question this way: "What will I sacrifice by choosing one option (***transformation***) over the other (the ***status quo*** of my practice, current level of competence, and confidence)?"

We provide some answers for you in **Table 7.2**.

Table 7.2: *Opportunity Costs—you can't have both columns*

Whichever column you choose, you get the whole column!	
Status Quo	**Transformed**
Quick "Fixes"	Planning, preparing, and participating in deeper learning requires adequate time for processing.

Comfort Zone	Not your entire comfort zone, but enough to examine your capability beliefs (expectancies of ability to achieve goals) and context beliefs (expectancies of responsiveness of environment to support goal attainment efforts). [Review Chapter 3 on personal agency beliefs.]
Comfort Zone	Again, not your entire comfort zone, but enough to step out and take some risks. This is the type of risk taking that is informed by current knowledge and skill level, supported by more knowledgeable others, and undertaken in a "safe" professional environment.
Lone Wolf Syndrome	You are part of a community of learners, and changes in your practice will affect others— teaching in isolation, learning in isolation, and problem-solving in isolation are all futile for the long-term.

It is a challenge to think of costs and what is left behind in terms other than negatives. Reframe your thinking to "trade-off" or "exchange for something better." Consider yourself to be a *wise* trader who anticipates and evaluates consequences, is prepared for delayed gratification, and **knows** *value* and *importance*.

The Monarch in The Analogy *traveled* a long way from having a broken heart "… for her people, isolated and without hope of visiting the neighboring islands to feast, explore, and learn new things" to

[a]nd then the Monarch truly understood the words of the Wise Advisor. *She saw that her subjects were much better subjects as she allowed them more freedom in how and where they traveled. In fact, she came to realize that the greatest gift she had given them was the freedom to explore and then appreciate their efforts, because they were successful at hard work. The*

resultant rewards her subjects received were much more valuable to them because of her willingness to empower them to do things on their own.

Her journey would have been short-lived had she not wrestled with the principles of reflective practice and opportunity costs for her choices. Additionally, she had to stay true to her vision (her *target*) of not only what she wanted for her subjects but also what kind of Monarch she wanted to be. Wise choices, informed choices, and ethical choices don't just happen. They are a result of purpose, intent, a determination to do good, and respect for those impacted by the choices.

Your choices will touch many lives. Be wise.

Figure 7.1. *Opportunity Costs: The Choice Is Yours.*

"He Said/She Said"

Dr. D: I've got a confession to make. Before I read this section, I was afraid we were going to get mired in a debate on the merits of reflection for evaluation. I'm pretty sure we won't convince teachers to welcome one more way to be evaluated.

Dr. J: Reflection has become a part of many teacher evaluation systems, but that's not what we are focusing on at this point. That is a whole other topic.

Dr. D: And this isn't some call to return to the *touchy-feely* 1970's reflection—right?

Dr. J: Hardly. We're talking about reflection that is self-imposed and involves true collegial interaction as the starting point.

Dr. D: What do you mean by "collegial interaction?" I remember some pre-school workshops that started with that term and ended up... Well, let's just say, once I was given a "warm fuzzy" to hand to another teacher by the end of the day.

Dr. J: No warm fuzzies! Teachers need a safe environment to struggle or wrestle with ideas. They need a sounding board for their thoughts. They also need opportunities to question their assumptions and perceptions about students, teaching, and learning. Colleagues can provide that safe environment. However, there must be the understanding that the purpose of the reflection and subsequent interaction with each other *is not* one consistent gripe session.

Dr. D: I get it. It's much easier to moan, groan, whine, and complain. The reality is: *that kind of communication quickly traps many teachers*. Their view becomes so skewed that any potentially profitable new understandings are complained away before given even a snowball's chance.

Dr. J: Yes, and that behavior also short circuits, or even blocks, the critical questioning and problem-solving process necessary for effective reflection. A teacher who commits to becoming a reflective practitioner needs *more knowledgeable others* in some form.

Dr. D: How do our teachers find those?

Dr. J: They could be other teachers with the same number of years teaching but more experience with specific content or subject-specific pedagogy; or teachers with more experience with a certain student population; or teachers of any tenure who regularly use critical thinking methods.

Dr. D: That's still a list of only teachers. What if a teacher is in a small school or department? There *must* be other options.

Dr. J: Most districts have educational leaders, department chairs, or administrators who have *personally* committed to reflective practice and value the potential reflective practice has to transform the educational environment. Those are also great places to start.

Dr. D: I know from personal experience that reflection of the type you've just described with colleagues who are on the same page is very invigorating. But, it's also important to point out that effective reflective practice can't be a one-time event. Periodic reflection is what makes the process worth the effort because it is the only way to produce *true* transformation.

Dr. J: You're right. It's a process. I want teachers to try it and then to describe what happened. I hope they'll pause to consider their feelings *and* the thinking *they used*. Evaluate influencing factors that led to their choices, actions, and perceptions. Analyze for opportunity costs. *Reframe, revise,* and *reconsider* what they're doing and how they're doing it based on their insights and learning. Then try again—take action!

Dr. D: I think I sense where you're headed. Let me lob another batting practice pitch to you: Wouldn't an excellent place to take the first step or sharpen reflective practitioner skills be in a *community of practice*?

Dr. J: [smiling] Perfect segue.

Invitation to Our Community of Practice

Challenge is a part of a teacher's life. Situations arise that are perplexing or frankly just frustrating. The "cup" at times may be overflowing, and not in a good way. Or, the "cup" at times may be overflowing with excitement about something new you have learned or a classroom success that you want to share with others. Another new policy or directive may just be the straw that breaks the camel's back, and you are looking for strategies or methods to help it all make sense. Or, you want to communicate and collaborate with others who will stretch and assist you move successfully along the novice to expert/master continuum from your current location to where you will be most effective. Reading our book was a step.

We are offering to be a part of your next steps by providing you a place to share your experiences in transforming common activities and implementing changes in your practice as a result of integrating elements of **Tune Up Your Teaching & Turn on Student Learning.** We offer you a place to discuss your professional concerns, questions, and needs.

Towards that end, we invite you to become a part of our community of practice through our website. It is a place where educators from all disciplines and levels of experience and expertise can *gather* around things that matter. *You* will help make it a place where shared concern around the teaching and learning environment provides the setting for you and others to learn together and create a pooled body of resources.

Join us. Because, when you cut to the chase, isn't the following quote something you'd like to hear from your students?

> Everyone who had you as a teacher [sic] are so happy that you challenged us so much cuz now [new] stuff is gonna be super easy.
>
> **KOC –** high school student

Example of Transforming an Activity

This activity, designed for and used by elementary students, was the end product of some time spent with Mrs. Dawn Himaka's Second Grade class. Dawn was one of Dr. Downing's students. She is an outstanding teacher who has been teaching from a *transformed* perspective for several years. Her students are the beneficiaries. However, all you secondary types, if you skip this transformed activity, you *will miss out* on an example of how reflective thinking among colleagues can benefit all involved.

Below is a list of the 3rd Grade California Science standards for Life Science from the **California Framework for Science Instruction** (1998, 12).

Life Sciences

1. Adaptations in physical structure or behavior may improve an organism's chance for survival. As a basis for understanding this concept:

    a. Students *know* plants and animals have structures that serve different functions in growth, survival, and reproduction.

    b. Students *know* examples of diverse life forms in different environments, such as oceans, deserts, tundra, forests, grasslands, and wetlands.

    c. Students *know* living things cause changes in the environment in which they live: some of these changes are detrimental to the organism or other organisms, and some are beneficial.

    d. Students *know* when the environment changes, some plants and animals survive and reproduce; others die or move to new locations.

    e. Students *know* that some kinds of organisms that once lived on Earth have completely disappeared and that some of those resembled others that are alive today.

The list of topics is just that—a *list*. The expected level of student learning is *knowing* (the italics in the standard are in the Framework document). You can all think of common assignments to deal with these, so we'll dispense with listing one here. At best, the common assignment involves **Engagement**.

Consider now the difference in the **Next Generation Science Standards (NGSS) for Grade Three**. © Copyright 2013 Achieve, Inc. All rights reserved.

Table 7.3. *California Grade 3 Life Science Standards*

3-LS2 Ecosystems: Interactions, Energy, and Dynamics		
Students who demonstrate understanding can:		
3-LS2-1. Construct an argument that some animals form groups that help members survive.		
Science and Engineering Practices	Disciplinary Core Ideas	Crosscutting Concepts
Engaging in Argument from Evidence	**LS2.D: Social Interactions and Group Behavior**	**Cause and Effect**
• Engaging in argument from evidence in 3–5 builds on K–2 experiences and progresses to critiquing the scientific explanations or solutions proposed by peers by citing relevant evidence about the natural and designed world(s). • Construct an argument with evidence, data, and/or a model. (3-LS2-1)	• Being part of a group helps animals obtain food, defend themselves, and cope with changes. Groups may serve different functions and vary dramatically in size *(Note: Moved from K–2)*. (3-LS2-1)	• Cause and effect relationships are routinely identified and used to explain change. (3-LS2-1)

Common Core State Standards Connections:

ELA/Literacy –

RI.3.1 Ask and answer questions to demonstrate understanding of a text, referring explicitly to the text as the basis for the answers. *(3-LS2-1)*

RI.3.3 Describe the relationship between a series of historical events, scientific ideas or concepts, or steps in technical procedures in a text, using language that pertains to time, sequence, and cause/effect. *(3-LS2-1)*

W.3.1 Write opinion pieces on topics or texts, supporting a point of view with reasons. (3-LS2-1)

W.3.9 Recall information from experiences or gather information from print and digital sources; take brief notes on sources and sort evidence into provided categories. (3-LS4-1)

The section entitled "Disciplinary Core Ideas" is reproduced verbatim from A Framework for K-12 Science Education: Practices, Cross-Cutting Concepts, and Core Ideas. Integrated and reprinted with permission from the National Academy of Sciences.

Source: Adapted from NGSS Grade 3.
©Copyright 2013 Achieve, Inc. All rights reserved.

Teaching for the 1998 standards aligns with what we've been calling *common assignments*. You can see that teaching for the 2013 standards requires transformed activities. The transformed lesson below is based on a model developed by Mrs. Himaka and Dr. Downing for the 1998 Standards.

Simply stated the model for this and other lessons includes a personalized scenario-setting story, a problem to solve, research to be conducted, and three types of writing prompts: an *informational* piece based on the research, a *narrative* piece—writing their own ending to the story, and an *opinion* piece—a campaign speech for their animal's "Very Best Animal in the Land" election campaign. Art is required in both the campaign poster and the poster of the animal in its native habitat.

Read through the edited version here. Look for evidence of the following Learning Tasks:

Analysis	Complex Tasks	Creativity	Curiosity	Engagement
Metacognition	Multiple Tasks	Persistence	Real World Tasks	Synthesis

Yep. We think they're all in here. Commentary by both Dr. Downing and Mrs. Himaka follow.

The Case of the Very Best Animal in the Land
By Mrs. Himaka and Dr. D.

It was another Monday morning at (1) School. All the students in Room (2) were ready for a great new week. Suddenly, as they were getting ready to go into their room, (3), cried, out, "Oh, my!"

"What is it?" asked (4).

"Are you hurt?" asked (5).

"Don't talk in line," said (6), always the one to be sure the rules were followed.

"Look!" was all (3) could say as she pointed toward a sign just outside the fence around the school.

Everyone in line turned like ducklings following after their mom.

"The sign's about an election," (3) shouted.

The whole class asked permission to go and investigate. (8) agreed that an investigation was needed. The teacher asked (10) to be the line leader and walk the class over to the fence.

What they found was very strange.

The sign said, "Vote Raccoon! for The Very Best Animal in the Land."

"But that's not right," (11) complained. "Raccoons aren't the best animals in the whole land."

"Sure they are," (12) said as she/he disagreed. "I think raccoons are cool. They even look like they're wearing masks."

"Just because an animal looks like a criminal doesn't make it the best anything," (13) said.

"But raccoons are criminals," (14) said. "At least my parents think they are."

"Why?" (11) wanted to know. "I think they're cute, not criminals!"

"I think it's time that we all take deep breaths," (8) interrupted. "Let's all go back to the classroom and do some planning."

Just then (15) came running up. She/He had not been in the line because she/he had been at the dentist office and was just a few minutes late to school.

"I saw a sign hanging on the school fence," (15) shouted. "It said, 'Everyone Likes Lizards. Vote Lizard!'"

"That's two signs," (16) said observantly. "It appears like there really is an animal election going on!"

… {content removed} …

Several minutes later (8) had a list of six reasons to vote on something written on the board. By that time (15) and (17) were back from taking pictures.

1. To elect a leader.
2. To decide on who looks the best when dressed up.
3. To decide who plays in an All-Star game.
4. To decide whose the best at something like singing or dancing.
5. To decide what kind of food to eat.
6. To pick a color, name, or subject for a project.

"I think this is an excellent list," (8) announced. "What should we do next? Talk with your table partners and come up with one idea." She/He let the class have time to talk and decide.

"It's time to move into our regular class agenda. Each person who is the Table Recorder this week, please write down your table's idea about what to do next and bring it to me. Tomorrow I will have all the ideas in a list…" she/he paused and looked right at (15) and smiled.

"And then we'll vote on what to do next?" (19) asked.

"That's exactly right! Tonight I want each of you think of a good reason for your table's idea what should be the first thing we do to find out why the animals are having an election."

That night, all the class members thought about why their table's idea should be first. They came to class the next day ready to share.

As the students arrived in Room (2) the next morning, the students were astounded when they saw, not one; not two; but *four* campaign posters on display in their classroom! [Authors' Note: These posters are in color in the purchasable activity.]

Besides the Raccoon's poster and the Lizard's poster, there were posters for Eagle and Spider. Each poster was spectacular and different from the others. All four together made an exciting sight! Room (2) looked like a place you see on television on election night.

(8) waited while the students inspected each of the campaign posters. <u>She/ He</u> was glad to see how interested the class was in the animal election. After a few minutes, <u>she/he</u> asked the students to return to their seats.

"(2) where did these posters come from?" (20) asked. "Animals can't write and draw."

"And *spiders* aren't even animals," (21) said. <u>She/he</u> was did not like spiders at all and did not want to have anything to do with them!

"Spiders are animals," (16) reported.

"They don't have hair," (21) stated.

"Neither do eagles," (15) answered. "They are birds, and they are animals."

"Well…" (21) thought hard. She/He didn't want spiders to be animals. Before she/he could come up with another reason, (22) gave her/his opinion.

"Spiders do not have bones," she/he said with authority.

"So they're not animals!" (21) said with relief.

"I'm afraid spiders are animals, (21)," (8) said, stopping the argument. "But what we need to do now is decide our first step in solving the mystery of the animal election. Take three minutes to share your reasons to support each of your table's idea. Choose one reason to present to the class."

… {content removed} …

The story isn't over yet. You get to help write the ending!

- Form three groups.
- Group **A** will research question 1 and question 6. [Authors' note: The questions are from the earlier list.] Group **B** will research question 2 and question 5. Group **C** will research question 3 and question 4.
- Each of you will write two sentences on what you think is a good answer for question 1, 2, or 3, whichever was assigned to your group. You will also write an *informational paragraph* as your answer to question 4, 5, or 6.
- Decide as a group your best answers to each question.
- Report your group decisions to the class.
- (8) will give you exact directions on the project you will do with the information.
- Once you complete your project, write the end to this story that you think is best.

The Best Animal in the Land:
An art and writing project on adaptations to the environment

Your job is to describe a "perfect" animal that inhabits the habitat assigned to you. No more than two people in a group can select the same animal as the "perfect" animal.

Your project will include a campaign poster with a slogan that could have a picture of your animal (like Eagle or Spider). On the back of your poster, draw a picture of your animal "where it lives." Include enough "background" in that picture so that it is obvious in which habitat your animal lives.

You will be writing a campaign speech for your animal using the answers to these questions about your animal and some of the "special adaptations" your animal has because of where it lives.

1. Write a definition of the word **adaptation**.
2. Finish this sentence: "My animal, the _(your animal's name)_, is the perfect animal for the _(name of habitat)_ because…(_write why here_).
3. Describe your animal. Tell what it looks like, list its special adaptations for survival (for example, a frog's webbed toes, a tiger's canine teeth), mention its animal group (mammal, reptile, amphibian, etc…).
4. Describe where it lives in the habitat. In which other continent or country would you find your animal?

… {content removed} …

HABITAT LIST:
- Southern California Chaparral
- Southern California Desert
- Southern California Foothills
- **Use the answers to your questions to help you as you complete the story and all the campaign materials.**

1.	2.
3.	4.
List the **Habitats** above and circle yours	
Write your campaign slogan below.	

Draw your animal's colorful campaign poster on one side of a blank sheet of white 8 ½" by 11" paper. And picture of your animal in its habitat on the other side of the paper.

> A complete version of this activity, which includes the editable story with color posters, a character list to personalize the story with student/teacher names from your class, writing templates and detailed teacher notes, is available from Mrs. Himaka's Teachers Pay Teachers website: http://www.teacherspayteachers.com/Store/Mrs-H-And-Dr-D.

Commentary. All of the requirements for the 2013 NGSS standards are not met in this example. However, you can easily add whatever pieces you (or your district/state) require at places you feel they are appropriate.

From Mrs. Himaka:

> "Animals" is a very engaging, high interest topic that all students are interested in learning more about. *Naming the perfect animal* is an argument even a **Kindergartener** could defend.
>
> In **Grades K-1**, students can learn about animal groups or specific animals. This teacher led beginning "research" can be noted or illustrated on posters or charts so that all students can access the information. Students can then *choose which animal they like the best or the animal they think is the strongest*. They can use the research generated to *defend why* they chose their animal and/or why they think it's the best or the strongest.
>
> In **Grades 2-3**, students can begin to *actively participate in the research* of an animal group or specific animal. They can perform research guided by the teacher or on their own, accessing information from the library, Internet, or nonfiction texts. Second and Third graders can then *state their opinion* of why a specific animal/group would be

more fit to survive in a specific environment or region. They could then *support or defend their opinion, citing facts from their research.*

In **Grades 4** and beyond, students could *conduct their own research*, citing many different sources and gathering facts and information, on a specific species, animal, environment and/or region. Their animal can then *participate in a mock election, deciding who is the most fit to survive* an environment/habitat/region. Students *create a campaign speech*, speaking as the specific animal, *defending their position* on why they should be the dominant or sole survivor of a specific habitat or region.

Integrating subjects not only creates a more interesting learning environment, it allows teachers to get a large amount of quality data and information on how a student actually performs and applies knowledge. This type of learning allows students to work cooperatively, learn from their peers and work at their own pace, *automatically differentiating the instruction.* It allows more time for those who require it while allowing those students ready to move forward to do so. This type of performance data and information is much more valuable than a percentage on a multiple-choice test.

Teacher Notes

- This story is designed for you to customize to your class. In the purchasable version, the file is a completely editable MSWord document saved in **.doc** format.
- The partial table that follows this paragraph is part of the list of *characters* in the story—essentially a MadLib© list. Names are indicated by bracketed numbers that correspond to the numbers on the MadLib© list. Write your students' names on that page, then replace the numbers in the story with the names. If you know how to search and replace, the process goes quickly. If you don't know how to use the Search/Replace feature, scroll through the story and change each (#) as you come to it.

Stu #	Mad-Lib© Description	Name in Story
(1)	**School Name**	
(2)	**Room Number**	**Room**
(3)	**Notices** *everything* **FEMALE**	
(4)	**Curious** FEMALE	

- At the end of the MadLib© list are blank spaces to allow you to include additional names in the story.
- After completing your customization, print the document (back to back if you want it to be like a book) and distribute the story to your class.
- Following the MadLib© list is an explanation of each of the three possible writing prompts you can use with the story. **If you just want to emphasize this as a science lesson on Animal Adaptations**, have your students complete only the research page in the text of the story. In the complete version, pages specific for each of the three Common Core writing requirements follow these notes.
- This integrated ELA/Science unit enriches and extends the topic of Animal Adaptations. (**See Table 7.3** for the actual standards.)
- Choose students who fit the description of each character in the story. If you run out of students, one student can play two roles. If you have more than the number of students in the story, find places where you might share a multiple-line speaking part.
- Enter the student names into the story.
- You may choose to print the one page of animal campaign posters in color so students can see it clearly. Photocopy the rest of the story.

*** IMPORTANT NOTE: Do not distribute the "Author's Ending". Make those copies separately and save until the very end.

- Your students will need resources or reference books (like a science book) to find the answers to the questions.
- Have groups share their findings with the class.
- Have students share their story endings in groups.

Common Core Integration Components

- At some point in the process, you will need to divide your class into groups and assign each group a different habitat. Each group will research the assigned habitat, taking notes as they do their reseach. (**CCSS.W.2.7** <u>Participate in shared research and writing projects</u> (e.g., *read a number of books on a single topic to produce a report; record science observations.*)

- Once the research is complete, have each student compose an informational paragraph using the information from their notes. (**CCSS.W.2.2** <u>Write informative/explanatory texts in which they introduce a topic, use facts and definitions to develop points, and provide a concluding statement or section.</u>)

References for Chapter 7

California Department of Education. 1998. California Framework for Science Instruction. Available: www.cde.ca.gov/be/st/ss/documents/sciencestnd.doc.

Chase, Betsy, Richard Germundsen, Joan Cady Brownstein, and Linda Schaak Distad. 2001. "Making the Connection Between Increased Student Learning and Reflective Practice." *Education Horizon* 48(3): 143-147.

Costante, Kevin. Interview with Richard Elmore. "Leading the Instructional Core: An Interview with Richard Elmore." *In Conversation* (11) 3. Summer 2010. Accessed December 9, 2013. http://www.edu.gov.on.ca/eng/policyfunding/leadership/Summer2010.pdf.

Danielson, Charlotte, and Thomas L. McGreal. 2000. *Teacher Evaluation: To Enhance Professional Practice*. Alexandria, Virginia: Association of Supervision and Curriculum Development.

Dewey, John. 1933. *How We Think: A Restatement of the Relation of Reflective Thinking to the Educative Process*. Chicago Illinois: Henry Regnery Co.

Downing, Charles, and Dawn Himaka. 2014. "The Case of the Very Best Animal in the Land". Used with permission: Teachers Pay Teachers website: http://www.teacherspayteachers.com/Store/Mrs-H-And-Dr-D

Elmore, Richard. 2008. "Improving the Instructional Core." Harvard University School of Education. Accessed October 13, 2013. http://sim.abel.yorku.ca/wp-content/uploads/2013/10/Elmore-Summary.pdf.

_____. 2009. "The (Only) Three Ways to Improve Performance in Schools". *Usable Knowledge*: Harvard Graduate School of Education. Accessed October 15, 2013. http://www.uknow.gse.harvard.edu/leadership/leadership001a.html.

Finlay, Linda. January 2008. " Reflecting on 'Reflective practice'". PBPL paper 52: 1-27. The Open University: Practice-based Professional Learning Centre. Accessed December 5, 2013. www.open.ac.uk/pbpl.

Killion, Joellen P., and Guy R. Todnem. 1991. "A Process for Personal Theory Building." *Educational Leadership* 48(7):14-16.

NGSS Lead States. 2013. *Next Generation Science Standards: For States, By States (Grade 3).* Washington, DC: The National Academies Press.

Schon, Donald. 1983. *The Reflective Practitioner: How Professionals Think in Action.* New York, New York: Basic Books, Inc.

Chapter 8

OUTLINED "CLIFF NOTES"©
OF THIS BOOK
LOOK HERE WHEN YOU'RE IN A HURRY!

Chapter Overview

This is a true overview of our book. If you remember, "I know I read that in the book," but you don't remember where—this is the place to start. We've pulled key topics from each chapter and placed them here, along with the section title where they are found. When our selection is not enough for your need, you can use the Table of Contents to quickly navigate to your desired location. The book ends with our last "He Said/She Said" and some quotes from teachers who learned how to **tune up *their* teaching and increased *their* student learning!**

Our Last Quote to Kickstart Your Thinking

> There are those select people one encounters in life that make you want to look, act and think as though you are far beyond your actual

> years... [The methods used in class] made me want to try hard not only in his class (which is the furthest thing from my actual life career goal) but try hard at all I did in school. He instilled a drive and a passion for me to pursue thoughts and ideas I would have never dreamt possible, and I almost always accomplished them... [H]e was the first instructor I encountered who held us accountable and responsible for doing our work and not letting us get away with anything...
>
> **JE** – University of Southern California

Briefest of Introductions

This is, as Captain James Tiberius Kirk famously intoned, "the final frontier." Well, actually it's just the final chapter, but that doesn't sound nearly as dramatic. The purpose of this chapter is to provide you with a quick reference point for locating information and ideas in the book. We've copied the overview of each chapter. We selected strategic subheadings from each chapter and copied/pasted key information verbatim below those subheadings.

Highlights of Chapters in Text or Tables

Chapter 1
Essential Questions

1. What is learning?
2. How do we design the learning environment so we hear statements such as "I learned how to think in your classroom because I had to," and, "I learned because you made me think."
3. How do we facilitate a change in students' expectations from "just tell me what to do" to "help me to learn how to think, so I can do it"?
4. What is the target? When students leave my classroom they will be____.
5. What type of thinking environment is necessary to reach the target? A thinking environment that is_____.
6. What does the teacher need to continue to do, and what does the teacher need to do differently?

7. What "basics" about teaching and learning do I need to consider for renewed study, professional reflection, and discussion?

Example of Transforming a Common Activity

This is listing key points on a topic.

- **Common**: Make a list with or without explanation.
- **Transformed**: Make a ranked list. Optional: Write a recruitment speech to a group who needs to know about that information.

Chapter 2
Teacher Roles

Table 2.1: *Teacher Roles and Categories*

Teacher Roles: General categories	Teacher Roles: Subcategories
1. Information provider	Lecturer; Clinical or practical teacher
2. Role model	On-the-job role model; Role model as teacher
3. Facilitator	Learning facilitator; Mentor
4. Assessor	Student assessor; Curriculum assessor
5. Planner	Curriculum planner; Course planner
6. Resource developer	Resource material creator; Study guide producer

Modified from Harden and Crosby (2000).

Student Roles

Table 2.3. *Generalized Roles Undertaken*
by Students and Characteristics of Those Roles

Student Roles	Characteristics
Receiver	I'll wait for you to give it to me.
Co-Constructor of meaning—sense-making	Can we think/do this together?
Independent inquirer/initiator	I am interested in knowing/trying more, and I will act.
Deliverer	I understand – let me tell/show someone else.
Resource	I am competent in this area. I'll be here if you need me.

Gradual Release of Responsibility Model

In building construction, adjustments are made to the scaffolding based on what has been completed and what is yet to be built. In GRRM, you do the same thing—adjust the scaffolding. Adjustments are based on knowledge of content, anticipated areas of difficulty, appropriate pedagogy for your student populations, and frequent, formative comprehension checks (Wood, Bruner & Ross 1976). Scaffolding is taken down once the structure is completed. It is superfluous—its purpose is "outlived." Your responsibility is also to take down the scaffolding when it's no longer needed. The goal is always the development of learner competence, personal responsibility, and accomplished independent practice and learning.

Keep the goal in mind. You want students who

- are independent learners with an enthusiasm for learning
- are engaged "in" learning
- understand, through experience, that learning is work
- have mastered content, developed functional and constructive cognitive, social, and emotional skills

- possess the ability to successfully synchronize all these attributes for achievement and success

Example of Transforming a Common Activity

This is collecting background information on a topic.

- **Common**: Lecture/Book as individual students.
- **Transformed**: Production of a "poster session" of the required information.

Chapter 3

Example of Transforming a Common activity

This is information gathering.

- **Common**: Finding answers to questions using the book or other resources.
- **Transformed**: Use the information from the question answers and progressively write: information pieces to complete sentences to a content-based narrative piece using the sentences.

The Elephant in the Room - Patterning of
Three Interacting Psychological Components

Table 3.2: *Summary of Motivation as Patterning*

Personal Goals	<ul><li>Goals have a motivational impact if they become *personal* goals.</li><li>A goal cannot truly be imposed on anyone. It must be adopted as a personal goal for it to perform a direction function—it either leads to a desired result or avoids an undesirable result (as cited in M.Ford 1992, 74; D.H. Ford and Lerner 1992, 181-182).</li></ul>

Emotional Arousal Processes	Ford makes a clear distinction between emotional and non-emotional affective states. Emotions provide evaluative information on the following: 1. Problems 2. Opportunities of potential relevance that the problems represent 3. Preparations that help the individual deal with problems and opportunities
Personal Agency Beliefs	Personal agency beliefs are defined as anticipatory evaluations about whether one can achieve a goal—the student's expectation of success. This motivational component is expressed through two processes, capability and context beliefs. It is the interaction of both types of beliefs that determines whether a student activates or inhibits behaviors that assist in attaining a goal.

A Summary of Sorts

Table 3.3a: *Motivational Systems Theory: Core Ideas (1)*

The Principle of Unitary Functioning	• One always deals with a whole person in context
The Motivational Triumvirate Principle	• Goals, emotions, and personal agency beliefs must all be influenced to facilitate motivation
Goals	• Little else matters if there is no relevant goal in place • Goals must be clear and compelling to transform concerns into intentions • Multiple goals can strengthen motivation substantially • Multiple goals must be aligned rather than in conflict to enhance motivation • Goals lose their potency in the absence of clear and informative feedback

Standards	• Flexible standards protect against demotivation and facilitate self-improvement • Challenging but attainable standards enhance motivation

Adapted from *Motivating Humans: Goals, Emotions, and Personal Agency Beliefs*; Martin E. Ford (1992).

TABLE 3.3b: *Motivational Systems Theory: Core Ideas (2)*

Emotions	• Strong emotions indicate and facilitate strong motivational patterns
Relationships	• Relationships are as important as techniques
Personal Agency Beliefs (PABs)	• Clear, specific evidence is needed to influence capability and context beliefs • PABs ultimately require real skills and a truly responsive environment • If a person is capable, just try to get them started
Change	• Incremental change is easier and safer • Transform only with care and as a last resort [Transform in this context refers to experiences that are dramatic and designed to shock, to escalate situations to a level that initiates sudden but dramatic change and must be reserved for extreme cases.] • There are many ways to motivate humans – if progress is slow, keep trying! • People must be treated with respect to produce enduring motivational effects

Adapted from *Motivating Humans: Goals, Emotions, and Personal Agency Beliefs*; Martin E. Ford (1992).

Chapter 4
The Balance of Challenge and Support

Challenge and support are companion elements that require careful and frequent assessment as to both quality and quantity. **Challenge** refers to a learning experience that requires a high level of independence and expectations—novelty is a valued component. Challenge is dependent on the knowledge and skill base of the learner as well as the features of the environment. In other words, an *appropriate challenge must be context-embedded.*

Support has many faces that are more process-oriented than content-oriented. Resources, materials, collaborative activities, and differentiated instruction all qualify as *support* when appropriately matched to the student and the learning task. A mismatch in any of these areas diminishes what *you intended as support.* Your mismatched effort becomes an obstruction or hindrance.

Just Manageable Difficulties

The most effective teaching and learning states occur within the ZPD that represents, for example, skills that are **slightly beyond** your students' demonstrated level of development. Without stretching your students beyond what they know they can do, development does not continue—your students cannot further develop on their own. However, with the guidance, support, encouragement, cooperation, and collaboration with *more knowledgeable others*—you or more advanced students—your students can develop to the next level.

Rigor

Rigor is the goal of helping students develop the capacity to understand content that is complex, ambiguous, provocative, and personally or emotionally challenging

(Strong, Silver, Matthew, and Perini 2001).

Categorizing and Leveling Thinking

Table 4.1b: *The Original and The Revised Bloom*

Original Bloom's Taxonomy (1956)	Revised Bloom Process Dimensions (2001)
Category/Level: *Synthesis* (noun) **Descriptor:** Put parts together to form a new whole	**Category/Level:** *Evaluating* (verb) **Descriptor**: Make judgments based on criteria and standards
Category/Level: *Evaluation* (noun) **Descriptor:** Judge value of material for a given purpose	**Category/Level**: *Creating* (verb) **Descriptor:** Put elements together to form a coherent or functioning whole; reorganizing elements into a new pattern or structure through generating, planning, or producing

- **See the complete DOK Chart online.**

Cognitive Rigor Matrix

We hope that we have convinced you of the value of analyzing the thought processes you require of your students. Stop reading, access the matrices, and begin the process. Remember, your goal is to provide balance across the categories of thinking in the matrix. *The goal is not to fill up the lower right-hand corner only*—there must be a balance between types of assignments and level of cognitive rigor required by your assignments and assessments.

Example of Transforming a Common Activity

This activity is about transforming an assessment.

- **Common**: Any assessment where the prompt is "Answer this direct question."
- **Transformed**: How to incorporate an open-ended prompt with an explanation of the concept of providing transitional prompts.

Chapter 5

Just How "Social" is the Social in Social Process?

The social environment of *school* includes more than who likes who, who gets along or doesn't get along with whom, what extracurricular activities are available, and how *we* as teachers prefer to configure our seating arrangements for individual or group work. When you restrict your definition of learning environment to the above, there will be problems. The research is conclusive—we are social beings and learning is influenced, enhanced, impacted, assisted, *and* encouraged by the quality of the social aspects of the teaching and learning environment.

Communities of Practice

Table 5.2. *Summary Statements about Communities of Practice*

CoP Summary
1. The process of learning and membership in a community of practice are inseparable. It is what lets us belong to and adjust our status in the group.
2. Communities develop around things that matter to people.
3. People organize their learning around the social communities to which they belong.
4. Knowledge is integrated in the life of communities that share values, beliefs, languages, and ways of doing things.
5. Real knowledge is integrated in the doing (the practice or ways of doing and approaching things that are shared to some significant extent among members), the social relations, and expertise of these communities.
6. A sense of joint identity and enterprise arises from organizing around particular activities and the general area of knowledge.
7. Members of a community of practice are involved in a set of relationships over time.
8. The interactions involved, and the ability to undertake larger or more complex activities and projects through cooperation, bind people together and help to facilitate relationships and trust.

Sources: (Ash 2010; Lave and Wenger 1991; Smith 2003; Wenger 2000).

Implications of Communities of Practice for Teaching

Transformation takes time. Intentional and purposeful choices and actions are required to develop a functioning *community of practice*. It requires a rethinking and re-orienting of teacher and student roles and an accurate understanding of the social principles of learning. Outside of school, students actively create or join communities to learn, practice, and produce resources and products for the benefit of the group. Unless your choices and actions integrate what students do naturally *outside of school*, transformation leading to formation of a community of practice is improbable.

Example of Transforming a Common Activity

This involves vocabulary or key terms in a unit of instruction.

- **Common Activity**: Define a list of terms…
- **Transformed Activity**: Production of catalogs of parts or terms by student groups.

Chapter 6
Novice to Master Continuum

Grant Wiggins puts this in perspective in his article "How Good Is Good Enough" (2013/14):

> *Knowing that you're a novice who's a long way from true mastery is not inherently debilitating. On the contrary, having a worthy, far-off goal and tracking your progress in closing the gap are key to mastery in all walks of life. (15)*

Focus on the Expert/Master Level

Research indicates that an individual must internalize and take action in four areas to achieve expert/master level. These areas are:

- an identification with a specific and *meaningful* goal or pursuit
- an *accurate* self-awareness of current levels of knowledge and skill as they *relate* to the ideal or target goals/performance

- a *desire* to persistently engage in the hard work required to conquer obstacles
- a commitment to *achieve* at optimal levels

Learners must have multiple opportunities to practice, have the time to practice, and be supported by formative feedback. Recall Bronislav, the apprentice, who worked under the watchful and committed "eye" of his master. He sought opportunities to demonstrate improvement over time. The master knew what the **end goal** was and that there were no shortcuts in the developmental process. A master's *role* is to provide an environment where each trial and error event is authentic and fuels both a reflective and a feedback/corrective process. There must be clarity by both the master and apprentice as to what constitutes excellence.

Since Practice Doesn't Necessarily Make Perfect, <u>What Type of Practice is Needed</u>?

One common characteristic in the four stages described in the novice to master continuum is *relevant practice in context*. This implies engagement and learning in authentic experiences. The learner takes on the identity of *practitioner* (recall Chapter 5 and importance of the practitioner identity). While simulations and other de-contextualized experiences may be practical and necessary in the beginning, at some point, the **real** has to be experienced if the *expert* or *master* label is to be achieved.

Deliberate Practice

Deliberate practice towards *expert* is not limited to performing a skill over and over again. According to K. Anders Ericsson (2006), a pioneer in research on *deliberate practice*, an expert also deconstructs complex tasks to specific skills. The expert then chooses which skills to focus practice on—those that need improvement.

Timely feedback is a companion to accurate self-analysis of performance. Necessary, also, is an increase in the level of challenge associated with the skill set being developed. A critical component is the individual's intent, commitment, and desire to actually master what is being practiced.

Mental Practicing

Practicing is an art, just as much as performing is, and practicing intelligently and in ways that derive the maximum benefit from our brains' natural abilities will only serve to enhance our artistry as [_____ fill in the blank authors' addition]

(Gebrian 2010)

Thinking as a practitioner—that is the key.

Example of Transforming a Common Activity

Eliminating extraneous materials from a problem's solution.

- **Common**: There is no common example.
- **Transformed**: There are two examples that are not content-specific.
  - Supporting a textbook on a tabletop.
  - Determining the volume of a golf ball.

Chapter 7
Teaching and Reflective Practice

Reflection has been viewed as a superficial and almost leisure activity—a passing fad in professional circles. Reflection can also be viewed as a disciplined process that is:

1. **Systematic**: regular, organized, efficient, logical
2. **Deliberate**: thoughtful, intentional
3. **Sustained**: persistent

The second view more closely characterizes what is termed *reflective practice*. One objective of reflective practice is developing a quality of reflection that allows for reproducibility of successes. *Effective* reflective practice recognizes serendipitous occurrences and the unexpected "ah ha" moments that help to shape new understandings and ways of addressing both content and pedagogy.

Opportunity Costs

This book is about *choices*. Throughout, we have asked and prodded and challenged you to make *choices*. The unspoken core question you may have asked yourself several times during your journey with us is, "What am I sacrificing?" Perhaps you expanded the question this way: "What will I sacrifice by choosing one option (***transformation***) over the other (the ***status quo*** of my practice, current level of competence, and confidence)?"

We provide some answers for you in **Table 7.2**.

Table 7.2: *Opportunity Costs—you can't have both columns*

Whichever column you choose, you get the whole column!	
Status Quo	**Transformed**
Quick "Fixes"	Planning, preparing, and participating in deeper learning requires adequate time for processing.
Comfort Zone	Not your entire comfort zone, but enough to examine your capability beliefs (expectancies of ability to achieve goals) and context beliefs (expectancies of responsiveness of environment to support goal attainment efforts). [Review Chapter 3 on personal agency beliefs.]
Comfort Zone	Again, not your entire comfort zone, but enough to step out and take some risks. This is the type of risk taking that is informed by current knowledge and skill level, supported by more knowledgeable others, and undertaken in a "safe" professional environment.

Lone Wolf Syndrome	You are part of a community of learners and changes in your practice will affect others—teaching in isolation, learning in isolation, and problem-solving in isolation are all futile for the long-term.

Invitation to Our Community of Practice

We are offering to be a part of your next steps by providing you a place to share your experiences in transforming common activities and implementing changes in your practice as a result of integrating elements of **Tune up Your Teaching & Turn on Student Learning!** We offer you a place to discuss your professional concerns, questions, and needs.

Towards that end, we invite you to become a part of our community of practice through our website. It is a place where educators from all disciplines and levels of experience and expertise can *gather* around things that matter. *You* will help make it a place where shared concern around the teaching and learning environment provides the setting for you and others to learn together and create a pooled body of resources.

Example of Transforming a Common Activity

- **Common**: This type of activity is common in all grade levels. Book work, worksheets, and coloring figures/maps on a topic is completed and that information is regurgitated as a product.
- **Transformed**: This activity uses a customized story, "The Very Best Animal…," for ELA/Science integration. Research results in the production of the Common Core writing prompts: *research*, *narrative*, and **informational**. Art assignments are a critical part of the final product.

"He Said/She Said"

Dr. D: I've been thinking. How many people actually read the Preface like we asked them to?

Dr. J: Why are you asking that at this point? They've finished reading the book.

Dr. D: Yeah, but the Preface is *really* good. And I think it's important that they know we did what we said we were going to do.

Dr. J: My hope is that everyone who read this book felt that we recognized and honored their perspective regardless of which of the four groups of readers we listed in the Preface.

Dr. D: Told you the Preface was important. [Smirking] You can only give one answer to this question: *What do you hope every reader takes away from our book?*

Dr. J: You first.

Dr. D: Okay. *I hope that every reader feels part of the passion in what we wrote and believes in its value.* If we accomplished that, *classrooms will be transformed.*

Dr. J: Yes, and each of those groups of readers ultimately influences what goes on in every classroom.

Dr. D: That was very profound. However, you can't dodge your answer anymore. Should I repeat the question? [Tapping foot while he waits.]

Dr. J: No, I got it the first time. At the beginning, we had ideas about what we wanted to do. It was important to me that we stayed true to our own experiences and years of privilege as teachers. So, my hope is that everyone who reads this book... it sounds so trite... but I am completely convinced that teaching is a calling. Those involved in the teaching and learning environment, individually and in community, *can bring about* the kind of transformation that is often only given lip service.

Dr. D: Beautifully stated; however, I think you've still managed to miss the *one* point you want them to take away.

Dr. J: Remember the map of Transformation Islands.

Dr. D: Yeah...

Dr. J: I hope that they know why we used *"We be here"* rather than *"Ye be here"*.

Dr. D: You might want to expand that just a bit.

Dr. J: At some point, we all begin on an island with no place to go and seemingly no way to get there. We are reluctant to travel beyond the comfort zone of our island shore. It's not so much that our hearts are not willing; it is more that we lose our direction in the whirlwind of educational fads, policy changes, and the day-to-day routines.

Dr. D: I think you've *almost* done it. Now... *what is your "final answer"*?

Dr. J: I want every teacher to take away this message: *Get back to the heart of the teacher.*

Dr. D: I like that answer. But I think I *want*, and I think our readers *need*, one more sentence of explanation.

Dr. J: What I mean is, I hope that every reader recognizes the amount of positive influence they have. Take that and now recommit to their practice and/or support of their students— whatever that means to each individual reader.

Dr. D: Tell it to them.

Dr. J: Do what you need to do. *Take from this book what you need to help you.*

The Real Last Words: Closing Quotes

You can do it. Kids can do it. But no one can do it without support, guidance, a starting point, and a plan.

O.M. – Teacher

Ok so from a teacher's point of view being in a [CoP] is wonderful because you are not on an isolated island. This is true and helpful especially for the beginning teacher. Everyone works together, shares their ideas, and the workload is divided! You are part of a team all working toward the common goal of helping kids be successful and engaged! As far as a school/parent point of view, there is a higher consistency. With [a CoP] there is accountability and consistency!!! This way everyone is on the same page.

J.M. – Teacher/Department Chair

Working in a collaborative group gives the opportunity to share ideas and/or best practices and devise ways to implement them. The creative energy from working in a group can be very powerful and meaningful. That reflects positively in the classroom.

C. H-S. – Teacher

INDEX OF FIGURES AND TABLES

Table Title

ABOUT THE AUTHORS

Dr. JoAnn Jurchan

Dr. Jurchan began her teaching career in elementary schools in 1979. She transitioned to teaching at the middle/junior high level where she designed a comprehensive junior high program for a K-8 school. Leadership positions held included vice-principal and lead teacher.

Additional teaching experience with GED and High School Diploma subjects in the Adult Education system provided an opportunity to teach at the high school level. In 1996, she accepted a teaching position at Granite Hills High School in alternative education programs for at-risk students. While there, she designed a high school independent contract credit retrieval program, coordinated school-wide literacy programs, was a member of the Literacy Professional Network, and was a San Diego County RISE trainer. From 2000-2003, she served as Founder and Director of the Eye of the Eagle Academies – a smaller learning community on the high school campus.

Dr. Jurchan earned a Masters in TESOL in 1999. She served as an adjunct professor in the Teacher Education Department of Alliant International University. In 2003, she accepted a position as an associate professor at Point Loma Nazarene University in San Diego, California. While at PLNU, she taught a number of Multiple Subject and Single Subject courses as well as Masters level courses. In 2004, she received a doctorate in Educational

Leadership. Her teaching career continues as an associate professor at Azusa Pacific University. Her responsibilities include teaching pre-service courses in the teacher credentialing program and overseeing the state teacher performance assessment program for the university.

During her career, Dr. Jurchan was honored with the *Greater San Diego Reading Association Award of Excellence*. She received the *Teacher of the Year Award* at Granite Hills High School. Dr. Jurchan was also the recipient of Azusa Pacific University School of Education *Excellence in Teaching Award*.

In addition to her teaching career, she served as Director of Educational Development for a national non-profit organization dedicated to providing K-6 systems with school-wide character education programs.

Dr. Jurchan is author of **Choices: Teacher's Resource Kit** (currently out of print) and contributing author to **Focus on Character. Character Counts!** Articles published in professional journals include: *Emotional Intelligence: An Introduction for the Educator, Dispositions in Teacher Education: Complex but Comprehensible* (co-authored), *The Case Study: Bringing Real-world Experience into the Teacher Preparation Program* (co-authored), and *Preparing Teachers to Support English Language Learners* (group-authored).

She has conducted numerous faculty trainings, presented, and consulted for state, national, and international audiences on a variety of critical education topics. Topics covered include, secondary content area literacy, universal access for diverse populations, second language acquisition theory and pedagogy, teacher dispositions, emotional intelligence, and the critical thinking approach.

Dr. Jurchan lives in the East County area of San Diego. Spending time attempting to outsmart gophers in her organic vegetable gardens takes up much of her leisure time.

Dr. Chuck Downing

Dr. Downing began his teaching career just as the huge body of the last T-Rex settled into the mud of a shallow Cretaceous Period sea. Actually, he began teaching high school biology in 1973 at Monte Vista High School in Spring Valley, California. After 23 years at MVHS, he received his doctorate and shifted his focus to working with preservice teachers, while still teaching some biology, at Point Loma Nazarene University in San Diego, California, where he as a full professor and Director of Teacher Education. After eight years in high education, he returned to his roots, finishing his teaching career at Great Oak High School in Temecula, California. He retired from full-time teaching in June of 2013.

During his career, Dr. Downing was honored as *San Diego County Teacher of the Year*, was a *Christa McAuliffe Fellow*, an *Access Excellence Fellow*. He also won the National Science Teachers Association's *CIBA-GEIGY Award* for innovation in high school teaching and received the *Presidential Award for Excellence in Secondary Science Teaching* from the National Science Foundation. He is the developer of six innovative laboratory and kinesthetic activities marketed by Science Kit and Ward's Biological Supply. His two-volume set of **Cranial Creations**, co-authored with both Owen Miller and Candace Aguirre, were best sellers for J: Weston Walch, Publishers. Most recently, he co-authored **AP* Biology Inquiry-Based Laboratory Investigations and Activities** with Linda Morris.

Dr. Downing now lives with his lovely wife, Leanne, and Hogan and Duke, two fine "rescue dogs," in the Point Loma area of San Diego. Still busy in retirement, he is the author of two science fiction books, **Traveler's HOT L**, and **The Observers**, published by Koehler Books as C. R. Downing. In addition to writing, he is active in ministry at Mission Church of the Nazarene. However, his favorite retirement activity is spending time with a very special miracle, his granddaughter Hadley Marie.

ONLINE RESOURCES

Depth of Knowledge (DOK) Information

A Guide for Using Webb's Depth of Knowledge With Common Core State Standards (Karen Hess, 2013):

http://cliu21cng.wikispaces.com/file/view/
WebsDepthofKnowledgeFlipChart.pdf/457670878/
WebsDepthofKnowledgeFlipChart.pdf

Webb's DOK Guide:

http://www.aps.edu/rda/documents/resources/Webbs_DOK_Guide.pdf

Webb's DOK Question Stems:

http://teachersites.schoolworld.com/webpages/hultenius/files/dok_question_
stems.pdf

Learner-centered Psychological Principles:

www.apa.org/ed/governance/bea/learner-centered.pdf

Engage in Thinking Website:

www.engageinthinking.com

Access Code for the Engage in Thinking Website <u>TuneUp.221</u>

REFERENCES

American Psychological Association Task Force on Psychology in Education. January 1993. "Learner-centered Psychological Principles: Guidelines for School Redesign and Reform." Washington, DC: American Psychological Association and Mid-Continent Regional Educational Laboratory.

American Psychological Association. November 1997. "Learner-Centered Psychological Principles: A Framework for School Reform & Redesign." Prepared by the Learner-Centered Principles Work Group of the American Psychological Association's Board of Educational Affairs (BEA).

Anderson, Lorin W., and David R. Krathwohl, eds. 2001. *A Taxonomy for Learning, Teaching and Assessing: A Revision of Bloom's Taxonomy of Educational Objectives: Complete Edition.* New York: Longman.

Ash, Doris. 2010. "Summary of Learning Theories-Cal Teach Program." ED 230 F2010 Reader. Accessed September 15, 2013. calteach.ucsc.edu/courses/.../Summary%20of%20*Learning*%20Theories.

Benner, Patricia. 1982. "From Novice to Expert". *American Journal of Nursing.* 82(3): 402-407.

Bloom, Benjamin S, M.B. Englehart, E.J: Furst, W.H. Hill, and David R. Krathwohl, eds. 1956. *Taxonomy of Educational Objectives: The*

Classification of Educational Goals, Handbook 1: Cognitive Domain. New York: Longmans, Green.

Brandt, Ron. 1998. *Powerful Learning.* Alexandria, Virginia: Association for Supervision and Curriculum Development.

Breen, Michael P., and Christopher N. Candlin. 1980. "The Essentials of a Communicative Curriculum in Language Teaching." *Applied Linguistics* 1 (2): 89-112.

Brim, Gilbert. 1992. *Ambition: How We Manage Success and Failure Throughout Our Lives.*

USA: Basic Books a Division of HarperCollins Publishers.

Brown, H. Douglas. 1994. *Teaching by Principles: An Interactive Approach to Language Pedagogy.* Upper Saddle River, New Jersey: Prentice Hall Regents.

_____. 2007. *Teaching by Principles: An Interactive Approach to Language Pedagogy.* 3rd ed. Pearson Education, Inc.

California Department of Education. 1998. California Framework for Science Instruction. Available: www.cde.ca.gov/be/st/ss/documents/sciencestnd.doc.

Chase, Betsy, Richard Germundsen, Joan Cady Brownstein, and Linda Schaak Distad. 2001. "Making the Connection Between Increased Student Learning and Reflective Practice." *Education Horizon* 48(3): 143-147.

Costante, Kevin. Interview with Richard Elmore. "Leading the Instructional Core: An Interview with Richard Elmore." *In Conversation* (11) 3. Summer 2010. Accessed December 9, 2013. http://www.edu.gov.on.ca/eng/policyfunding/leadership/Summer2010.pdf.

Csikszentmihalyi, Mihaly. 1990. *Flow: The Psychology of Optimal Experience.* New York: Harper & Row.

_____. 2008. *Flow: The Psychology of Optimal Experience.* New York: Harper Perennial Modern Classics.

Csikszentmihalyi, M. and Barbara Schneider. 2000. *Becoming Adult: How Teenagers Prepare for the World of Work.* New York, New York: Basic Books.

Daley, Barbara J: 1999. "Novice to Expert: How Do Professionals Learn?" Adult Education Quarterly 49(4): 133-147.

Danielson, Charlotte, and Thomas L. McGreal. 2000. *Teacher Evaluation: To Enhance Professional Practice.* Alexandria, Virginia: Association of Supervision and Curriculum Development.

Dewey, John. 1933. *How We Think: A Restatement of the Relation of Reflective Thinking to the Educative Process.* Chicago Illinois: Henry Regnery Co.

Downing, Charles, and Dawn Himaka. 2014. "The Case of the Very Best Animal in the Land". Used with permission: Teachers Pay Teachers website: http://www.teacherspayteachers.com/Store/Mrs-H-And-Dr-D

Downing, Charles, and Marquand, Marilyn. 2000. "Tune up Your Teaching." Unpublished manuscript. Available online at http://www. engageinteaching.com.

Dreyfus, Stuart, and Hubert L. Dreyfus. 1980. "A Five-Stage Model of the Mental Activities Involved in Directed Skill Acquisition." Supported by the Air Force Office of Scientific Research (AFSC), USAF, under Contract F49620-79-C-0063 with the University of California, Berkeley. Unpublished study. February 1980.

_____. 1986. *Mind Over Machine: The Power of Human Intuition and Expertise in the Era of the Computer.* New York: The Free Press.

Duvivier, Robert J:, Jan van Dalen, Arno M. Muijtjens, Véronique Moulaert, Cees van der Vieuten, and Albert Scherpbier. 2011. "The Role of Deliberate Practice in the Acquisition of Clinical Skills." *BMC Medical Education* 11: 101.

Elmore, Richard. 2008. "Improving the Instructional Core." Harvard University School of Education. Accessed October 13, 2013. http://sim. abel.yorku.ca/wp-content/uploads/2013/10/Elmore-Summary.pdf.

_____. 2009. "The (Only) Three Ways to Improve Performance in Schools". *Usable Knowledge*: Harvard Graduate School of Education. Accessed October 15, 2013. http://www.uknow.gse.harvard.edu/leadership/ leadership001a.html.

Ericsson, K. Anders, Neil Charness, Paul J: Feltovich, and Robert R. Hoffman, eds. 2006. *The Cambridge Handbook of Expertise and Expert Performance.* Part of Cambridge Handbooks in Psychology.

Finlay, Linda. January 2008. "Reflecting on 'Reflective practice'". PBPL paper 52: 1-27. The Open University: Practice-based Professional Learning Centre. Accessed December 5, 2013. www.open.ac.uk/pbpl

Ford, Donald H. 1987. *Humans as Self-Constructing Living Systems: A Developmental Perspective on Behavior and Personality.* Hillsdale, New Jersey: Lawrence Erlbaum.

Ford, Donald H., and Richard M. Lerner. 1992. *Developmental Systems Theory: An Integrative Approach.* Newbury Park, California: Sage.

Ford, Martin E., and Donald H. Ford, eds. 1987. *Humans as Self-Constructing Living Systems: Putting the Framework to Work.* Hillsdale, New Jersey: Lawrence Erlbaum.

Ford, Martin E. 1992. *Motivating Humans: Goals, Emotions, and Personal Agency Beliefs.* Newbury Park, California: Sage Publications.

Gawande, Atul. 2011. "Coaching a Surgeon: What Makes Top Performers Better: Personal Best." *The New Yorker: Annals of Medicine*: 9-16.

Gebrian Molly. 2010. "What Musicians Can Learn about Practicing from Current Brain Research." Accessed November 10, 2013. http://madisonjazz.files.wordpress.com/2010/05/practicingandcurrentbrainresearchbygebrian.pdf

Harden, R.M., and Joy Crosby. 2000. "The Good Teacher is More Than a Lecturer: The Twelve Roles of the Teacher." *AMEE Guide* 22: 334-347. Accessed July 5, 2013. doi:10.1080/014215900409429.

Hektner, Joel M., and Mihaly Csikszentmihalyi. 1996. "A Longitudinal Exploration of Flow and Intrinsic Motivation in Adolescents." Paper presented at the Annual Meeting of the American Educational Research Association, New York, New York. April 8-12.

Hess, Karin K. 2006a. "Applying Webb's Depth-of-Knowledge (DOK) Levels in Science." Accessed November 10. http://www.nciea.org/publications/DOKscience_KH08.pdf.

_____. "Exploring Cognitive Demand in Instruction and Assessment." Accessed November 10. http://www.nciea.org/publications/DOK_ApplyingWebb_KH08.pdf.

Hess, Karin K. 2012. "A New Lens for Examining Cognitive Rigor in Assessments, Curriculum, & the Common Core: Connect the Dots:

Implementing & Assessing the Common Core Standards." Presentation at Wisconsin ASCD Meeting, Madison, Wisconsin, January 11, 2012.

Hess, Karin K., Dennis Carlock, Ben Jones, and John R. Walkup. 2009. "What Exactly Do 'Fewer, Clearer, and Higher Standards' Really Look Like in the Classroom? Using a Cognitive Rigor Matrix to Analyze Curriculum, Plan Lessons, and Implement Assessments." Presentation at CCSSO, Detroit, Michigan, June 2009. Available online: http://www.nciea.org/cgi-bin/pubspage.cgi?sortby=pub_date.

Hobbs, Nicholas. 1974. "A Natural History of an Idea." In *Teaching Children With Behavior Disorders*: Personal Perspectives, edited by J.M. Kaufman & C. D. Lewis, 145-167. Columbus, Ohio: Charles E. Merrill.

Kessler, Rachael. 2000. *The Soul of Education: Helping Students Find Connection, Compassion, and Character at School*. Alexandria, Virginia: Association for Supervision and Curriculum Development.

Killion, Joellen P., and Guy R. Todnem. 1991. "A Process for Personal Theory Building." *Educational Leadership* 48(7):14-16.

Krashen, Stephen D: 1982. *Principles and Practice in Second Language Acquisition*. Oxford: Pergamon.

_____: 2004. *The Power of Reading: Insights From the Research*. 2nd ed. Portsmouth, New Hampshire: Heinemann.

Lave, Jean, and Etienne Wenger. 1991. "*Situated Learning. Legitimate Peripheral Participation*." Cambridge: University of Cambridge Press.

Locke, John. 1690. *An Essay Concerning Human Understanding*. Digireads.com, 2008.

_____. 1693. *Some Thoughts Concerning Education: And, of the Conduct of the Understanding*, edited by Ruth W. Grant and Nathan Tarcov. Indianapolis, Indiana: Hackett Publishing 1996.

NGSS Lead States. 2013. *Next Generation Science Standards: For States, By States (Grade 3)*. Washington, DC: The National Academies Press.

Pascual-Leone, Alvaro, Dang Nguyet, Leonardo G. Cohen, Joaquim P. Brasil-Neto, Angel Cammarota, and Mark Hallett. 1995. "Modulation of Muscle Responses Evoked by Transcranial Magnetic Stimulation During the Acquisition of Fine Motor Skills." *Journal of Neurophysiology* 74(3):1037-1045.

Pearson, P. David., and Margaret C. Gallagher. 1983. "The Instruction of Reading Comprehension." *Contemporary Educational Psychology* 8: 317–345.

Pena, Adolfo. June 2010. "The Dreyfus Model of Clinical Problem-Solving Skills Acquisition: A Critical Perspective." *Medical Education Online 2010*; 15:10.3402/meo.v15i0.4846. doi: 10.3402/meo.v15i0.4846.

Penner, D:, Nancy Giles, Richard Lehrer, and Leona Schauble. 1997. "Building Functional Models: Designing an Elbow". *Journal of Research in Science Teaching* 34 (2): 125-143.

Polanyi, M. (1966). *The Tacit Dimension.* Univeristy of Chicago Press.

Potts, Bonnie. February 1994. "Strategies for Teaching Critical Thinking." ERIC/AE Digest. ERIC Clearinghouse on Assessment and Evaluation, Washington, DC. ED385606.

Rosenberg, Marc. 2012. "Beyond Competency: It's the Journey to Mastery that Counts." *Learning Solutions Magazine.* Accessed November 15, 2013. http://www.learningsolutionsmag.com/articles/930/beyond-competence-its-the-journey-to-mastery-that-counts.

Sagor, Richard. 2002. "Lessons from Skateboarders." *Educational Leadership* 60(1): 34-38.

Scherer, Marge. 2002. "Do Students Care About Learning? A Conversation with Mihaly Csikszentmihalyi." *Educational Leadership* 60 (1): 12-17.

Schon, Donald. 1983. *The Reflective Practitioner: How Professionals Think in Action.* New York, New York: Basic Books, Inc.

Smith, Mark K. 2003. " 'Jean Lave, Etienne Wenger and Communities of Practice,' *The Encyclopedia of Informal Education.*" Accessed October 8, 2013. www.infed.org/biblio/communities_of_practice.htm.

Strong, Richard W., Harvey F. Silver, and Matthew J: Perini. 2001. *Teaching What Matters Most: Standards and Strategies for Raising Student Achievement.* Alexandria, Virginia: Association of Supervision and Curriculum Development.

Sun, R., Robert C. Matthews, and Sean M. Lane (2007). "Implicit and Explicit Processes in the Development of Cognitive Skills: A Theoretical Interpretation With Some Practical Implications for Science Instruction.

In Elizabeth M. Vargios ed., *Educational Psychology Research*:1-26. New York: Nova Science Publishers.

Sutman, Francis X, and Others. March 1993. "Teaching Science Effectively to Limited English Proficient Students." ERIC/CUE Digest, Number 87. ERIC Clearinghouse on Urban Education, New York, N.Y. ED357113.

Tomlinson, Carol Ann. 2013/2014. "Let's Not Dilute Mastery." *Educational Leadership* 71(4): 88-89.

Venditti, Phillip. 2001. "A New Motivational Principle for Educators." *Educational Horizons* (Winter): 85-88.

Vygotsky, Lev S. 1978. *Mind in Society: The Development of Higher Psychological Processes*, edited by M. Cole, S. Scribner, V.J: Steiner, and E. Souberman. Cambridge, Massachusetts: Harvard University Press.

Walker, Matthew P., and Robert Stickgold. 2005. "It's Practice, with Sleep, that Makes Perfect: Implications of Sleep-Dependent Learning and Plasticity for Skill Performance." *Clin Sports Med* 24: 301-317. This work was supported by grants from the National Institutes of Health (MH 48,832, MH 65,292, MH 69,935, and MH 67,754) and the National Science Foundation (BCS-0121953).

Wang, Ming Te, and Jacquelynne S. Eccles. 2013. "School Context, Achievement Motivation, and Academic Engagement: A Longitudinal Study of School Engagement Using a Multidimensional Perspective." *Learning and Instruction* 28: 12-23.

Webb, Norman L. 1997. Research Monograph Number 6: "Criteria for Alignment of Expectations and Assessments on Mathematics and Science Education." Washington, D:C.: Council of Chief State School Officers from the National Science Foundation.

_____. August 1999. Research Monograph No. 18: "Alignment of Science and Mathematics Standards and Assessments in Four States." Washington, D:C.: Council of Chief State School Officers from the National Science Foundation.

_____. 2002 "Depth-of-Knowledge Levels for Four Content Areas." Unpublished paper. March 28, 2002.

Webb, Norman L. and others. "Web Alignment Tool." 24 July 2005. Wisconsin Center of Educational Research. University of Wisconsin-

Madison. 2 Feb. 2006. Accessed November 8. http://www.wcer.wisc.edu/WAT/index.aspx.

Webb, Norman L. 2009. "Webb's Depth of Knowledge Guide: Career and Technical Education Definitions." Available online: http://www.aps.edu/rda/documents/resources/Webbs_DOK_Guide.pdf.

Wenger, Etienne. 2000. *Communities of Practice: Learning, Meaning, and Identity.* Cambridge University Press.

Wenger-Trayner Website [Beverly Wenger-Trayner & Etienne Wenger-Trayner]. "Intro to Communities of Practice." Last modified 2011. http://wenger-trayner.com/theory/.

_____. "Communities Versus Networks?" Last modified Posted by Team BE Dec. 28, 2011. http://wenger-trayner.com/resources/communities-versus-networks/.

_____. "What is a Community of Practice?" Last modified Posted by Team BE Dec. 28, 2011. http://wenger-trayner.com/resources/what-is-a-community-of-practice/.

_____. "What is Social Learning?" Last modified Posted by Team BE January 1, 2012. http://wenger-trayner.com/all/what-is-social-learning/.

Wiggins, Grant. 2013/2014. "How Good is Good Enough?" *Educational Leadership* 71(4): 10-16.

Wood, David, Jerome S. Bruner, and Gail Ross. 1976. "The Role of Tutoring in Problem Solving." *Journal of Child Psychology and Psychiatry* 17(2): 89–100.